PRAISE FOR *THE YOU PLAN*

The shame and pain of divorce is so great that women are tempted to make desperate and destructive decisions that can greatly compound the pain of divorce. Thus, every divorced woman needs a plan. This is the plan you need. Michelle and Connie provide an effective plan to help you heal and get your life back, but even better.

—STEVE ARTERBURN, FOUNDER, NEWLIFE
MINISTRIES AND WOMEN OF FAITH; AUTHOR,
THE 7-MINUTE MARRIAGE SOULTION

The YOU Plan is a detailed roadmap for women navigating the personal and circumstantial landmines of an unexpected divorce. Lost and scared, you face the unknown with feelings of rejection, fear, guilt, shame, and unworth. At this vulnerable time, you need other women who have walked this path and successfully come out the other end. Michelle and Connie provide just that roadmap, openly sharing their journeys and tackling the tough but crucial lessons they've learned along the way. If you're stuck and scared, but are ready to move forward, *The YOU Plan* will help you heal--one step at a time.

—LESLIE VERNICK, COUNSELOR,
COACH, AUTHOR, AND SPEAKER

In a world where living authentically is overlooked and undervalued, Michelle and Connie provide a roadmap to help women heal and move forward. Through their authentic and transparent writing women will feel like they are not alone. Michelle and Connie encourage women to feel empowered and hopeful by addressing key struggles that they go through after divorce. There is no "elephant in the room" with this book. It is refreshing, encouraging, and authentic.

—SHARON K.B. DALE, LPC MHSP,

co-author, *DIVORCE TO WHOLENESS*

THE
YOU
PLAN

THE
YOU
PLAN

A CHRISTIAN WOMAN'S GUIDE

FOR A HAPPY, HEALTHY LIFE AFTER DIVORCE

MICHELLE BORQUEZ
AND CONNIE WETZELL

NELSON
BOOKS

An Imprint of Thomas Nelson

Published in Nashville, Tennessee, by Nelson Books, an imprint of Thomas Nelson. Nelson Books and Thomas Nelson are registered trademarks of HarperCollins Christian Publishing, Inc.

Thomas Nelson, Inc., titles may be purchased in bulk for educational, business, fundraising, or sales promotional use. For information, please e-mail SpecialMarkets@ ThomasNelson.com.

Published in association with MacGregor Literary, 2373 N.W. 185th Avenue, Suite 165 Hillsboro, OR 97124-7076; macgregorliterary.com.

Names and identifying details of some people mentioned in this book have been changed to protect their privacy.

The websites recommended in this book are intended as resources for the reader. These websites are not intended in any way to be or to imply an endorsement on behalf of Thomas Nelson, nor does the publisher vouch for online content for the life of this book.

Unless otherwise cited, Scripture quotations are taken from the *Holy Bible*, New International Version®. Copyright © 1973, 1978, 1984, 2011 by Biblica, Inc.™ Used by permission of Zondervan. All rights reserved worldwide. www.zondervan.com.

Scripture quotations marked NASB are taken from the NEW AMERICAN STANDARD BIBLE®, © The Lockman Foundation 1960, 1962, 1963, 1968, 1971, 1972, 1973, 1975, 1977, 1995. Used by permission.

Scripture quotations marked NLT are taken from the *Holy Bible*, New Living Translation. © 1996, 2004, 2007. Used by permission of Tyndale House Publishers, Inc., Wheaton, Illinois 60189. All rights reserved.

Scripture quotations marked NKJV are taken from THE NEW KING JAMES VERSION. © 1982 by Thomas Nelson, Inc. Used by permission. All rights reserved.

Scripture quotations marked ESV are from the ENGLISH STANDARD VERSION. © 2001 by Crossway Bibles, a division of Good News Publishers.

Library of Congress Cataloging-in-Publication Data

Borquez, Michelle.
 The YOU plan : a Christian woman's guide for a happy, healthy life after divorce / Michelle Borquez and Connie Wetzell.
  pages cm
 Includes bibliographical references and index.
 ISBN 978-1-4002-0551-6 (alk. paper)
 1. Divorced women--Religious life. 2. Christian women--Religious life. I. Title.
 BV4596.D58B67 2014
 248.8'433--dc23

2013025272

Printed in the United States of America

13 14 15 16 17 RRD 6 5 4 3 2 1

From Michelle:

To women who are hurting from the aftermath of divorce, women whose hope has been shattered and whose light has dimmed. My prayer is you not only receive healing from what Connie and I have shared, but you are given renewed vision for your life.

You are valuable. You are accepted. You have purpose. May the Lord give you strength as you walk out the process of wholeness in your life.

From Connie:

I would like to dedicate this book to all the dear souls who have had their hearts broken and dreams demolished from the devastation of divorce. Even though you will never forget this significant chapter of your life's journey, one of my deepest desires is for you to develop new dreams, for you to heal and move forward in the full intent and purpose that God has for you with joy. May YOU press on!

CONTENTS

FOREWORD

Malachi records this declaration from God: "'...I hate divorce,' says the Lord, the God of Israel" (Malachi 2:16 NASB).

Since His creation of the first man and woman in the garden, God's design was for one man to be married to one woman for one lifetime. Married in a relationship that was covenanted with Him, and committed to each other "till death do we part."

But we live in a broken world. And divorce happens.

Many reading this right now didn't even have a say in what happened. But the pain is real and the road to new life isn't easy.

As the president of the nearly 50,000 member American Association of Christian Counselors, and the executive director of the Center for Counseling and Family Studies at Liberty University, I have come to a heartbreaking conclusion—there is no such thing as an "easy" divorce.

Emotions are bruised.

Hearts are shattered.

Love is crushed.

Children get hurt and confused.

Families are torn.

But . . . you can get through this.

Tragically, in my experience, I have found that a lot of women never truly heal from the trauma of divorce. They too often self-medicate, and even run to a "new" relationship, simply to try to forget the betrayal, anger, pain, unforgiveness, and fear that consumes them every waking moment.

A friend who had experienced a difficult divorce said to me, "I want to get my 'bounce' back." To which I replied, "You will—but only after you have healed—don't short circuit the journey!"

And healing is a journey. A journey that requires a plan.

In *The YOU Plan*, Michelle and Connie not only explain that journey, they offer to walk through it with you. The way in which they portray their own mistakes, highlighting real life experiences and pointing out their own sometimes "off-road" journey, will help you avoid the pitfalls that could potentially lead to more heartache and chaos, and further delay your healing. Every chapter has a checklist of thoughts, a plan of action, and a prayer of reflection.

While it is true that God hates divorce, it is also true that neither "height nor depth, nor anything else in all creation, will be able to separate us from the love of God in Christ Jesus our Lord" (Romans 8:39 ESV).

Not only does God love you with an everlasting love—He still has a plan for your life—and He *knows* the plans He has for you (Jeremiah 29:11). You are not defined by your divorce. You are defined by your relationship with a loving, gentle Abba-Father whose love for you and toward you is still intact. A plan that is not hidden from you, but is hidden for you. The finding is in the journey.

The You Plan is written specifically to help you navigate your way back to the life God desires for you. A life that is whole . . . healed . . . and holy.

There are no coincidences in the kingdom of God. You picked this book up for a reason. You may be reeling from the pain of a recent divorce. Or perhaps your divorce was years ago, but you just can't seem to get back on track. The resource you hold in your hands can help facilitate the work that God wants to do, and can do, in and through you.

The real issue is, are you going to press into Him?

It's time to start the journey.

Dr. Tim Clinton

President, American Association

of Christian Counselors

WHERE WE ARE NOW

We may never get over the effects of divorce, but most divorced women do get over the feelings of hopelessness, despair, anger, worthlessness, shame, guilt, and many of the other emotions we all feel when we are walking through the devastation of divorce. It doesn't feel like it at the time, but your heart will heal, and you will live, laugh, and maybe even love again. We are living proof of this truth.

You *will* heal. But we don't want you to delay the healing process because of bad decisions or choices. Discovering a happy, healthy life after divorce is a process. You can't just go through a drive-through window to pick up a certificate of healing. Wouldn't it be lovely if you could? While there is no quick fix, there are steps to becoming a whole and healthy new you. Wholeness is the key to life after divorce. There is a huge hole in your heart, and you are seeking ways to fill it.

While we are not in any way coming from an expert viewpoint, we have a lot of experience in rebuilding happy, healthy lives after divorce. Our desire is that you, too, will arrive at the door of a whole new you sooner rather than later.

Both of us, Connie and Michelle, are here to provide support to the many Christian women who are working through the muck of divorce. We have personally walked this road with many women who are hurting and working to heal from the aftermaths of broken marriages.

The more we have worked with women, the more aware we have become of the importance of giving women a road map to navigate their lives after divorce. Like driving a car on an unfamiliar path, we encounter many ditches, roadblocks, and accidents after divorce. Without some form of direction and a navigating system, it can seem hopeless. But the two of us are far down that road and are able to journey with you if you will allow us. As we open up our hearts and share what we have learned and overcome, we hope you will be encouraged and have the tools you need to avoid some of the pitfalls along your way.

FROM "HOLENESS" TO WHOLENESS

Michelle

The entire first year after my divorce, I could barely lift my head off the pillow. It took everything I had to get my kids to school, put together a meal, or feel any sense of hope. I think the statement "Divorce is like open-heart surgery with no anesthetic" is true. Like any surgery, the recovery process is also up to you. You can go right back out, start living recklessly, and be in the hospital again having to go back under the knife, or you can listen to and heed the advice of people who are safe and whom you trust.

I have to admit I went off-roading a few times after my

divorce, and believe me, I didn't like one moment of it. Connie and I both would love the chance to do it over again and focus on the right things instead of the things that are able to destroy us.

I was longing, searching, looking for a way to fill the hole in my heart, a hole that felt as big as Texas. When I walked around, I felt people could see right through it, as if I were half a person. I have to admit, my mind and heart could not fathom even the possibility of feeling whole again. It just didn't seem possible at the time.

Can you relate? Are you still in the place of feeling totally hopeless? It's okay. You may live there for a while, but we don't want you to stay there. We want you to move beyond the hurt and hopelessness when it's time. Unfortunately, you have to walk through the pain to get to the other side. There is no avoiding it. It's inevitable. No one wants to feel pain, but the process of denial pushes you into reality at some point. I remember many times waking up feeling as if my divorce was just a bad dream. None of it was real. It couldn't be. There was no way my marriage could be over—and yet it was. I didn't want a divorce, so dealing with the reality was even harder to accept.

My dreams, my hopes, my life, and even my identity were tightly woven within the parameters of my marriage. Divorce was a foreign concept to me. With no divorce in my family and not knowing even one couple who had gone through a divorce, I was totally clueless how to navigate my post-divorce life. I had no role model to look to, no success story of someone who had moved on and her life had turned out okay. I just knew I wasn't okay, and I had no idea if I ever would be okay again.

Being a positive and optimistic person by nature, this new place of despair and hopelessness was something I didn't want to be familiar with. I knew self-medicating, running from, or—for lack of a better word—partying to avoid my pain would not help. I had lived that life as a young girl and knew it led to emptiness. But after my divorce I spent a whole year angry at God and felt justified in my anger.

I was angry because I felt that after becoming a Christian I had lived the "right" life. I had done all the "right" things. I was a leader in ministry, dedicated to sharing the Word of God. I had a checklist of all the things I had succeeded at doing. My failed marriage didn't make sense to me. Was there something I missed? The Christian journey is not about a walk of performance, a walk without trials or tribulation; it's about entrusting our lives to Christ no matter what. It took me a year of pressing through my anger, disappointment, fear, and pain to get to the place where I finally was ready to fully surrender my heart to Jesus despite the unmet expectations, the perceived failure, and the loss of my marriage and my dreams. It wasn't easy, but I finally got there.

In the meantime, during that year, the Lord never left me. He met me in my pain. He pursued me even in my unfaithfulness. Have you been unfaithful to God? Are you angry with Him? I understand, and so does He. Being honest with your feelings is the most important step. We will talk about that in this book.

What inspired me to write this book was looking back at my own lack of direction as I grappled to figure out how to live again. It wasn't easy learning how to be single, how to be a mother to four kids without a husband to help, how to provide financially and still be present in my kids' lives, how to do simple chores like fix things around the house, and eventually how to date again. It was hard to sleep alone, to cook for just the kids and me, and it took me forever to remember to set the table for five instead of six. Sometimes the loneliness seemed so unbearable I didn't know if I could go on.

If it wasn't for the love of my children, I am not sure I'd be here. They were amazing through everything. I am grateful for their love. I never criticized their dad. I encouraged them to love him and to ask God's forgiveness for any feelings of anger toward him. I stressed over and over again to my children the importance of forgiveness, yet forgiveness for me took quite some time. I was so angry with him. I was angry with him for causing hate to rule in my heart for a season—a hurdle I had to overcome.

I always share with women that the first thing you want to do after a divorce is look at yourself. Focus on changing you, making *you* better, and that is exactly what I focused on. I worked hard with a counselor for several years to get beyond my anger, disappointment, and fear. It wasn't easy to resurrect old wounds and work through them, wounds from my childhood that I had never addressed. You may be thinking, *What do wounds of my childhood have to do with my divorce or where I am today?* When you go through a divorce, you become completely vulnerable. In this state of emotional brokenness, it's easy for old wounds and insecurities to resurface if you haven't taken the time to work through them. After my divorce, I felt like a teenage girl who had been rejected. I felt unworthy all over again. It wasn't easy to dig up the issues of my past and work through them, but I knew the importance of wholeness, and I did not feel whole. If I ever wanted to be married again, I knew how important it would be for me to be healthy in every way. I wanted to be the best me I could be, even if that meant working through some very painful memories.

I also wanted to look at areas of my own heart I felt were unknown to me until my divorce. I talked with a counselor about feelings that had surfaced and thoughts I had fought with. It was healing to be able to walk through the shame, guilt, and anger with someone safe. My perspective as I began working through these things changed over time. It's easy for unhealthy mindsets to form as a result of pain.

Those who have journeyed the road after divorce are all too familiar with the painful journey back to wholeness—and some, unfortunately, never get there. They get stuck in unforgiveness, anger, or guilt and never move beyond these feelings to the freedom awaiting them. The process is painstakingly gut-wrenching, yet there are great moments of gratitude and tremendous leaps of forced growth. The hole in your heart right now will one day truly be made whole.

During my single years, it was hard to travel alone. I had to carry my own bags, drive myself to the airport and back, and spend many nights eating alone. Yet after a few years of intense counseling and exhaustion from my continued fighting against the aloneness, I realized that there is wholeness in aloneness when you accept it.

That is where I am today. My journey has been one of walking out the healing, learning to forgive, and focusing on what is in front of me instead of staying stuck in the past. I've had to learn some things the difficult way because I had no one to walk me through the process with wisdom. I had to navigate the mucky waters of divorce completely alone. I knew no one who could give me the advice I needed on dating, being a single mom, and dealing with the ache of loneliness.

I survived, and so will you. And I not only survived, but I am now thriving in wholeness and happiness once again. It's not the perfect life, but it's a mended life, a life redeemed. God truly does redeem the broken pieces of our lives. And I'm not talking about being remarried. I found my wholeness in God before my new husband and I married. God completes us, and a husband is truly icing on the cake.

Today, I am free from guilt, shame, agony, and the fear of the bottom falling out once again. I am free because I have come to learn that no matter what happens, no matter how bad life can be, God will never leave me nor forsake me. He has seen me through the most desperate of times, and He will do the same for you.

My husband, Michael Thornton, was not on my radar. Yet God knew that one day we would be together. We had been friends for twelve years and my brother Tony and Michael were good friends for many years. Because of the way we were introduced, I really saw him like a little brother.

I had come to the place of accepting I may never marry again. My expectations were so high I knew it would take a miracle to find someone I could have faith in again. I couldn't even imagine what it would be like to trust someone with my heart. It seemed so foreign to me. Seven years is a long time, and I had adjusted to being single. Michael and I had a long-term friendship that usually involved us getting together for dinner or just to hang out a few times a year. He lived in Texas, and when I was there for a short time, I gave him a call to get together—and that night he chose to share his heart with me.

What was different this time was that I had not tried to go out and find someone to fill the void. The void was filled by God. I simply went about my life, and there Michael was, standing in front of me. I really believe God chose that time for me. It wasn't planned or even a forethought, and suddenly God brought us together for a greater purpose, to be difference makers. This is my heart, and to be with someone whose heart identifies with mine, and really gets me, is an overwhelming gift.

Michael is great with my four children. He is truly a blessing in my life, and for the first time I feel I am alive and engaged in a mutually beneficial relationship. It's a beautiful season.

Many divorced women look to my life as a source of hope, but the truth is, the hope we are all searching for is in Christ. Put your hope in Christ, and the outcome will be a sense of peace. Connie and I can offer you a road map, but you will still have to get in the car and drive in the direction we are suggesting. I would have loved to have someone's help in navigating through the wreckage after my divorce, but overall, while I did some off-roading there for a time, I am thankful for the journey and feel stronger and wiser for it.

Most of all, the wholeness I have experienced as a result of my surrender in the pain and suffering is definitely something I would never trade. To know God is real and to watch His hand move in my life because He loves me unconditionally is more than my mind can fathom.

SINGLE BUT NOT ALONE

Connie

Almost ten years ago, I was going through a divorce, the empty, nest syndrome, a milestone birthday, and perimenopause all at the same time. That's enough to drive any woman off the deep end. I remember sitting in a corner of the house alone and rocking back and forth for about three days wondering what I was to do next. I wrote about this in *Live, Laugh, Love Again*.[1] In that book my girlfriend cowriters and I walked through the stages of grief and the rocky road from divorce into singleness.

Okay, fast-forward. Here we are ten years later, and Michelle and I decided to put our heads together to share some of our experiences about life after divorce. We'll tell you what we've learned and give you a few pointers in the hope that you don't make some of the mistakes we did. It's not that we're experts. Neither of us claims to have the magic pill to a perfect life. It's just that we've "been there, done that" and learned a few things in a very painful way. We'd like to spare you that pain if we can. But I find that even though most of us instinctively know the right thing to do, sometimes we have to bail our way out the hard way before we learn the lesson. And many of us have to go through getting our hearts broken more than once. I'll be the first to raise my hand and admit that's me.

So here I am, approaching another milestone birthday. Menopause came and went. I'm still single. And guess what? I'm okay with that. It's not my preference. I would still love to meet the right guy for me, but if it doesn't happen, I'll be fine. Maybe it's not in God's plan for me to remarry. Maybe I'm just supposed to remain single. Being single has many incredible perks, one of them being that you have the freedom to make all your own decisions. I've also learned that there is absolutely no perfect scenario in life—no matter what. You could be married to the hottest guy in the universe with more money than you know what to do with, all the kids you've ever dreamed of, and a Halle Berry body, and you know what? You'd still want something more. I've also learned that the more you have, the more you have to worry about. And it's far worse to be trapped in a marriage to Mr. Wrong than to be single.

Since my divorce, I have been in a couple of very serious relationships that ended badly and left me brokenhearted again and again. And I had a slew of other short-term relationships that disappointed me in some way or another. I will elaborate on those relationships in this book. You see, I really needed to take time to heal after my marriage of twenty-six years ended. But did I do that? No! I got right back in the dating game, thinking I was just fine and ready to go for it. It's like when you have an injury and you get a cortisone shot that makes you feel better. But all it does is mask the pain. The injury is still there. So you're still using that muscle/joint/bone/tendon, hence doing more damage to it. The injury gets worse and worse, and you don't realize it until the cortisone shot wears off. *Ouch!* I began to realize that I'm terrible at picking out good men for me (note that I didn't say the men were bad; they just weren't the right fit for me), and I attracted the wrong type of men. That's what usually happens when you're not emotionally healthy. So I've been on a dating hiatus since 2010 trying to get healthier, and hopefully will have a better shot at doing it right the next time if the opportunity comes up. Let's just say I'm open to it.

One thing I did realize is that I don't like being alone. It's not that I don't like being *single*; I don't like being *alone*. I was never alone my entire life until Fred left ten years ago. I was always used to being around family and friends regularly. I went from high school to college and dorm life, then immediately to married life and children, so I had no idea what it was like going solo.

A few years ago, I had an aha moment. I was doing a speaking engagement in the St. Louis area, and I decided to visit my second cousin, who is a nun, at the convent in Ruma, Illinois. I hung out for the day and spent the night at the convent. I began to see that the nuns had a very cool thing going on. They ate together, played games together, prayed together, and went out in the community and helped others. They had a vegetable garden they planted and tended to. The women were there for each other. But each nun had her own private quarters if she needed some alone time. If not, she could hang out with the other sisters. I loved it.

As I was walking around the lake at Ruma, I saw a nun who was way up in years on her knees picking weeds. As a matter of fact, many of the nuns were elderly. I asked her if she would mind telling me how old she was, and she proudly told me she was ninety-three. I asked what her secret was for staying so youthful and active. She replied something like this: "Well, we're married to the best—Jesus!" (Each sister wears a gold wedding band on her left hand to signify her covenant with Jesus.) She went on to say, "And if there's a problem in our relationship, it's our fault." She laughed and then continued, "We don't have children to worry about. We don't have financial woes. The church takes care of us. We eat together, pray together, play games together, shop together, help others, and we're there for each other. We have a great community. If we want to be alone, we can go to our rooms. But if we need someone to lend an ear or pray with us or laugh with us or cry with us, there's always someone there."

Immediately, I thought, *What a brilliant idea! I need to round up six to eight of my girlfriends. We're going to build a house that has a lovely living room and kitchen area, let's say in Hawaii. It will have private quarters for each of us with our own entrances. And we're going to call it the Con-Vent. (Get it? A play on Connie.) My friends could live with me, "Con," and then we could "vent" anytime we want. And we wouldn't be alone. Anyone want to sign up?* I have mentioned this idea to several of my single girlfriends, and they're all ready to sign on the dotted line because it sounds so wonderful.

As I continued healing, I was able to see the many blessings and benefits of my life. For one thing, my work brings me great satisfaction and flexibility. As a self-employed voice-over artist and writer, I can work remotely. Because of this luxury, I'm able to travel when I want to, which allows me to spend ample time with family and friends. I'm truly blessed and don't take it for granted.

One of the other joys in my life is being a *nonna* ("grand-mother" in Italian) to two of the sweetest boys on the planet. Can I just say that I'm gaga over my grandsons? There is this place inside you that is untouched and undiscovered, and you don't know it exists until you see your grandbaby. And then a feeling wells up inside you, a love you've never felt before, and you are hooked for good. So for now, my grandsons are the two main men in my life.

Both of my daughters are strong women who have gone through life's triumphs and tragedies. But I continue to see in every situation the truth of Romans 8:28: "God causes all things to work together for good to those who love God, to those who are called according to His purpose" (NASB). And I can say with all my heart that God listens to the cries of a praying mother, indeed. Don't ever give up praying and believing for your children.

As I mentioned earlier, I still have hope that someday the right man for me will come along. It is one of my heart's desires. And why wouldn't it be, since God wired us to be in relation-ships? Even though I'm very rich in friendships and have plenty of social interaction, it is not the same as having that special someone who is there for you when you need him most. That someone lying down beside you at night (but, please, God, don't let him snore too much). The one who is there for you when you don't feel well, who will cuddle with you, pray with you, or get you what you need. That someone you can talk to in the morning and have your first cup of coffee with. However, in my singleness, I have found that God has always provided for my needs in every way. His plans are good, whether single or married.

Now that I have finally taken the time to heal, have taken a long look in the mirror, and have gone through some extensive counseling, I feel that I'm in a much better place. God knows the deepest desires of my heart. I trust Him to give me exceedingly and abundantly more than I'd ever hoped or dreamed.

• • •

Enough about us, let's talk about you. Let's get busy helping make a YOU plan that will take you toward your goal of living a life that will bring purpose and joy.

one

THE REAL LIFESTYLE LIFT

t's the latest fad. This lifestyle lift only takes an hour, and out
you walk, looking younger, wrinkle free, and just a tad different. It's a whole new you. Wow!

Wouldn't it be great if you could walk out of your divorce and
get a lifestyle lift? Not plastic surgery, but a makeover that would
completely transform your pain, sorrow, and new reality into
joy, happiness, and a whole new you? Transforming a life after
divorce is much more difficult than transforming an aging face.
While the idea of getting older can take its toll on some, it's definitely not the same in terms of what you have to deal with being
newly divorced.

A forty-year-old face as opposed to a twenty-year-old face
is much easier to accept than the idea that your husband no longer wants you, cares about you, or even desires to be in the same
room as you. While both are harsh realities we must face, the
solutions are totally different.

So what are the first steps of a real lifestyle lift? Most of us
are pretty low to the ground after our divorces. For some it would

take a construction crane to lift them out of bed. It's okay; Connie and I (Michelle) have been there and understand. It's not easy to have the reality of where your life has landed staring you in the face every day. Not to mention the constant painful reminders and memories you have to deal with, among a slew of other things.

Where does this journey to wholeness begin? How do we move from pre-lifestyle lift to the real deal? Skipping the steps to wholeness is like getting a face-lift from someone who is not a doctor. It will end up being a botched job, and those are not fun. You can't make over your life overnight, and you certainly cannot skip the steps necessary in the process of moving toward wholeness.

We are here to help you navigate the steps and to walk through this journey with you. You are not alone. We cannot say that too many times. You no longer have to feel like you are in the hospital waiting room, staring into space, wondering what the process of rebuilding your life is going to be like. We are here to give you the inside scoop that will hopefully keep you from any possibilities of a botched recovery. The last thing we want is for you to have to go through more pain, damage, or grief. We are here to lift you up and walk with you.

Step one of the journey is acceptance. Yep, it's accepting the reality of where you are right now with the understanding you are just passing through. You won't stay in the stages of shock and grief, so hang in there. Remember, be patient and realize there is no quick recovery.

To see where you are on your journey toward acceptance, answer these questions:

1. Are you still living in the past?
2. Do you find yourself dwelling on things your ex did?

3. Are you still trying to figure out who was wrong?
4. Do you look for ways to get revenge?
5. Do you feel you have unhealthy boundaries with your ex?
6. Are you harboring resentment or bitterness?
7. Are you seeking out a relationship or new marriage to replace your ex?
8. Do you find yourself self-medicating or demonstrating extreme behavior?
9. Do you feel stuck or in limbo?
10. Do you look for ways to find out what your ex is doing, even if it means using the children?

These are just a few questions to get us started. If you answered yes to any of them, acceptance is still something to continue working toward. It's definitely not easy. When we say it's a process, we mean it's a process. Some of you will never fully accept what has happened, but if you can at least move beyond it and begin getting healthy, it will be a huge step in the right direction. The moments of not accepting reality will become fewer and fewer. It seems hard to imagine now, but you will get there. We definitely felt just as you do right now. The mountain in front of you seems almost impossible to climb, but you must go over it or you will remain stuck, and this is where resentment and bitterness can take root.

Every day you spend living stuck in your past, stuck in your unforgiveness and bitterness, is a day you are taking away from you, your family, and those who you love and are closest to you. But no one just walks out of a divorce and is "fine." The initials for "fine" in your situation most likely mean *frustrated, insecure, narcissistic,* and *emotional,* and you have every right to be—at least until you can find the strength to accept where you are and begin to take the steps to wholeness.

Holding on to unforgiveness is like drinking poison and hoping the other person dies. It hurts only you. Accepting, forgiving, and leaving the outcome of your life in God's hands is what helps you more than anything to get to a healthy place so the "holeness" and emptiness you feel right now will be exchanged for wholeness.

BABY STEPS TO WHOLENESS

Michelle

It took me a year to accept the fact that my marriage was over. At first, I couldn't grasp that what was happening to me was not only very real but forever life changing. I remember many mornings waking up wondering if it was all just a bad dream. I'd look around my room and then remember what my reality truly was. It was so heartbreaking. I cried for two years after my divorce. I didn't know so many tears could come out of one person. I didn't think I could ever feel normal or whole again.

It's all about taking small steps toward the wholeness you desire. I talk to women weekly who have been through or are in the process of divorce. My heart aches for them, and I wish so badly I could just pick them up and move them to the other side of their heartache, but there is no way around it, no way under it, no way over it. You can only go through the pain to get to the other side, one step at a time.

What did moving through the pain look like for me? Not having anyone to help me navigate through the muck was difficult. I was very much naive to the process and went on instinct. It is really about getting to the place where you are willing to say, "Okay, I accept this situation, as unjust as it is. Lord, I surrender it all to You regardless of the outcome. I trust You with my life, my heart, my children, and my future." This is so difficult to say, yet the first step to moving toward wholeness is accepting and trusting God in the process.

Divorce is not final when the papers are signed and delivered. The outcome and consequences are never ending. There are those few who never see each other again; but for those who have children and those whose marriages were their very identities, their lives were intertwined on so many levels, a divorce is just the beginning of a long life of sorting through issues and managing children, property, and anything else related to the marriage.

I received an e-mail from a woman about her divorce. She and her husband were closely intertwined financially, personally, and even in the community. They owned a chain of health clubs together, were well known in their community, and had been married for thirty-five years. He met a girl not much older than their oldest daughter at their place of business and fell in love. I could go on to tell you the details of this relationship, but I will spare you the agony. After the divorce was over, instead of his life falling apart and him losing everything, he continued to prosper—at least for now. I do believe wholeheartedly that you will reap what you sow.

Even after several years of their divorce being final, her ex marrying the girl who worked for them at their business, not to mention the many affairs he'd apparently had during the marriage, this woman was still struggling with acceptance. She didn't want him back—if he had asked, she would never have taken him back. But she had difficulty accepting this was her life. Accepting she was alone. Accepting she no longer had someone to go to sleep with at night, to help with the kids, to hold her, to feel the strength of. Accepting the possibility of dating again if she wants to be with someone—something that to a newly divorced person is frightening.

I felt the same way about dating as this woman. I even hated dating when I was a young single girl—the whole process of going on a date, seeing if there was any compatibility between the two of you, and then finding a way to tell the person you weren't interested, or vice versa. Dating is not something we suggest you do right away, but this is one of the first things newly divorced people tend to do. However, we stress that if you have not yet reached the stage of acceptance of your divorce, then dating is absolutely the last thing you should do.

I had people trying to set me up with Prince Charming. I was so broken inside and was in no shape to carry on a conversation, much less a relationship; but I found myself going down that path just to have some adult company. While Connie and I want you to get to the place of acceptance, we definitely don't associate acceptance with dating again. Well-meaning people may encourage you to "move on," yet in your heart you are not ready to do that. You can barely move.

It took me years to get to the place of acceptance. I had moved on in every way—new man, new car, new life—yet my heart was still in a million pieces. What I should have done was allowed my heart to heal and then allowed my healed heart to lead me forward, realizing that changed circumstances were not going to take away the pain or the reality of my life.

Oh, how I wish—oh how Connie and I both wish—we would have had someone helping us navigate through the decisions!

That's why we are writing this book. We desire more for you and want you to be as successful as possible in walking through one of the most devastating circumstances you may ever have to face. Onward we go!

GOD, GRANT ME THE SERENITY

Connie

If you've ever gone to any kind of addiction meetings, they often say the Serenity Prayer: "God, grant me the serenity to accept the things I cannot change, the courage to change the things I can, and the wisdom to know the difference." You are not only asking God for His help to accept the tough stuff life brings your way that you can't change, but you are also asking Him to bring you a sense of peace in the midst of it. This peace is achieved when we decide to surrender to God. It's going past the bargaining stage of grief. (The five stages of grief are Denial, Anger, Bargaining, Depression, and Acceptance.) When you realize you can't change what is and understand that God is in control and He is sovereign, you can experience peace. Surrendering produces the serenity you're praying for. It's trusting God explicitly that everything's going to be okay. That He's going to take you to a better place.

Have you gotten there yet? Have you faced the fact that you're divorced . . . that your husband is not coming back? Have you faced the fact that the dream you had can't be fulfilled any longer? Are you looking at your reality? Are you looking at the cards you're holding? Because you need to be at that place before you can move on to the next step. The good news is that there are things you *can* change. But they don't have anything to do with changing anyone else. Change is about you and comes from within. When you've arrived at the land of acceptance, you're able to begin carving out a new life for yourself.

Let's say you are lost, and you want to get to my house. So you call me and ask for directions. I ask you where you are, but you don't know. If you don't know where you are, how can you find your way to my house? Sometimes it's too foggy or the storm is too blinding. You can't see well enough to know where you are. Don't fret. Soon you will see clearly and be able to find your way.

Acceptance is the opposite of denial. That's why denial is the first stage of grief, and acceptance is the last. When something major occurs in your life, particularly a loss, it takes some time to come to terms with what has actually happened. You have to grieve your loss before you can ever get to the place of acceptance. Let yourself feel from the depths of your soul. The only way to get to the acceptance stage is to be totally honest with yourself about what is, not what was or what you hoped would be. Acceptance is the beautiful doorway to new hopes, dreams, and possibilities. It brings peace, healing, and freedom.

I can only speak from experiences in my own life. I remember when my husband left. He moved out of the house for a month before he made his decision to file for divorce, and the entire month he was gone, I prayed and believed that he'd change his mind and come home. I kept thinking that I was in an ugly nightmare. Surely I would wake up and find him next to me. But after he filed for the divorce and I was served the papers, I knew I wasn't dreaming anymore. He wasn't coming back. Gone was my dream that we'd grow old together. That we would be a close-knit family, and our kids and grandbabies would be in church together followed by a big Sunday dinner at our house. Birthdays and Christmases all together would not be.

That dream died, and I had to face my new reality. I tormented myself with all the lies: *I'm not good enough, pretty enough, this enough, that enough,* or *I'm too much this, that, or the other.* Through prayer, counseling, and being loved and nurtured by good friends, I finally was able to accept the truth about myself and my situation. I didn't like where I was, but realizing the truth opened the doorway to new things. And I'm here to encourage you. If you're taking the right steps to take care of yourself, you will get to a happy, healthy place all in good time.

Let's fast-forward ten years. That's how long it has been since my divorce. Here is my new reality. I am a divorced woman, currently not in a relationship with another man. I spend a lot of time being alone, though I do much better when I'm around people regularly because I'm a people person by nature. I've just celebrated another decade birthday, and as a woman who deals with anxiety issues, this one was tougher because the window of my life is getting smaller. My two grown daughters have gone through more heartache and pain than many women their age ... some because of the choices they've made in their lives and some because of circumstances out of their control. The four people I love the most in my life, my two daughters and my two grandsons, live twenty-four hundred miles away from me. They live in the same city their dad and the woman he left me for live. My children and grandchildren get to see his wife more than they get to see me. It took me some time to come to terms with this. Do I like it? No, I don't. That's the way it is, though.

But here is the other side of my reality. I am a single woman living in a great city. I don't have any family members here, but

I am exceedingly wealthy in relationships because of all the incredible friendships I have. I attend a wonderful church. I'm in good physical health, thank God, which is why I was able to celebrate another birthday. I love the work I do. God has blessed me with the flexibility of being able to work from anywhere in the world. This affords me opportunities to go frequently to the city where my children and grandbabies live for extended periods of time and have quality visits with them. My daughters are doing much better. I firmly believe this is because God is so tender toward the prayers of a mother's heart. My grandsons are crazy about me, and no one can ever take my place in their lives. I am in a position where I can choose to move where they are or continue to go back and forth between the two cities.

I told you all this because I want you to see the cards I was dealt. There were some tough cards in my hand: singleness, living alone, kids dealing with major stressors, bouts of anxiety, which is a far cry from the debilitating panic attacks I suffered from years ago, being far away from my family, and the hurt of the kids and grandkids seeing Fred's wife, Wilma, more than they see me.

Now let's look at the good cards: close friendships, living in a great city, a wonderful church, good health, a job I love, the flexibility to work anywhere, beautiful daughters for whom I see God is answering prayers, sweet grandsons, and being able to go back and forth between two cities. My good cards outweigh my bad cards.

When I can see the full hand by accepting the good and the bad of what is, I can proceed to change some of the situations that are not desirable. I will not be able to change all of them, but some of them I can.

It dawned on me the other day that the reason I've had such a difficult time accepting my new reality is because of the expectations I had for my life. When I was a much younger woman, right after I accepted the Lord at the age of twenty, I went to college on a music scholarship and sang with an incredible show band. Life was good. I loved my school. I loved the kids on campus. I loved music. I loved being young and free. I remember saying, "I'm going to meet a fabulous man with all these certain qualities, we're going to fall deeply in love, I'll be married before the age of twenty-five, I'll have two children before I'm thirty, and life will be almost perfect. We won't have financial problems, and we'll all be in church and live the great American dream. I'll be a stay-at-home mom with a perfect house and home-cooked meals every night. We'll have a beautiful family and lots of friends." And do you know what? It happened just as I said it would. Everything fell right into place.

But the divorce wasn't part of the story I'd written out for myself. In fact, it changed everything else about my story. I've cried enough tears to fill Lake Michigan. I've worried to the extent of having to repent of it frequently because worry has become somewhat of an idol. And I've prayed my guts out asking God why. My friend, it's just life. Everybody has their stuff. All you can do is pray and love God with all your heart, do the next right thing, and then stand in full surrender. Stand on the Word. Stand on His promises. Stand next to Him. When you stumble, He holds your hand and dusts you off and helps you get back up. And with His help, you put one foot in front of the other and keep going.

I'd like to tell you about a couple of friends of mine. Jan had been living a vibrant life with her very successful husband. She had been experiencing some pain and numbness, and after a series of tests, she was diagnosed with a neurological disease. Instead of looking at how bad that could be, she looked at what she had going for her and became proactive in managing this disease. I rarely hear her talk about her disease, and she's always doing something that makes a difference in other people's lives or pursuing things she loves, like writing and art. She's approaching her seventies and still sees a world of possibilities in front of her. She works with her illness and doesn't let it dominate her life or define who she is.

I have another friend, Karen. Karen has been successful for much of her life. She was an entertainer for a long time, created her own magazine, and is an optimist. After her husband passed, she was diagnosed with an arthritic condition that keeps her hobbling around much of the time. She uses a cane and sometimes even a scooter to get around. Karen loves to travel, and she hasn't let her condition stop her from doing what she loves. She has been all over the world in the last fifteen years, by herself, and she's seventy-six years old. She always has a smile on her face.

Both Jan and Karen accepted their reality and played the good cards to create happy, healthy lives. Their debilitations don't dominate their lives. That is the common ground between both these friends. They're upbeat and positive. I love associating with people who have this attitude. Debbie Downers don't work well for me. That doesn't mean that I don't want to listen to, support, or pray with a friend having a bad day or walking through a painful situation. I'm talking about those people who always walk around with a chip on their shoulders. They're always the victim. It's unhealthy to be around people like that.

In the Serenity Prayer, we ask for wisdom. It's one of the finest things we can ask God for. The Word of God tells us that if we pray for wisdom, God will surely give it to us: "If any of you lacks wisdom, let him ask of God, who gives to all liberally and without reproach, and it will be given to him" (James 1:5 NKJV). This is a promise we can count on.

So I leave you with this visual. Imagine a beautiful bracelet with these links: *forgiveness* links to *acceptance*, which links to *surrender*, which links to *serenity*—and all these things link to *a happy, healthy life*.

And please take heart. It doesn't matter what your circumstances are now or how old you are. Life is full of options at every stage.

YOU and Acceptance Thoughts

Have you accepted where you are so that you are able to begin moving ahead? Or are you still living in a state of denial, unable to face the future? Regardless of your answer, we are here for you, ready to help you navigate through it all. We understand how difficult it is to reach acceptance, and in no way are we condemning you by asking where you are in your journey. We realize acceptance is a process. It won't happen overnight; it takes years to move through the healing and the forgiveness, believing and trusting that God has you in His hand. Our hope is that you will recognize where you are and then begin the process of baby steps toward acceptance. One foot in front of the other, and soon you'll be walking through the door.

YOU and Acceptance Actions

So what are some steps to begin the acceptance process? How did you do on the acceptance test we gave you earlier? Let's evaluate some of the questions and then address some things that might be helpful for you to move ahead.

Are you still living in the past?

This is definitely something you have to ask yourself every day: *Am I living in the past?* You will constantly deal with memories, places, and thoughts that remind you of the life you once lived. Here are a few strategies to help you move beyond the past into a new future:

- Stay away from old hangouts for a while.
- For a season don't listen to songs that are reminders of your past.
- Begin to create new memories with your friends or your kids. Purposely do things that will be memory creating. Take photos and post them around your house to remind you of the new life you are living.

Do you find yourself dwelling on things your ex did?

- Instead of thinking about what he did, think about how you could have added more value to the marriage, ways you could have handled things differently. Ask yourself questions about how you can become better through all you have had to go through.

- Make a list of all the things your ex did and then ask yourself what control you have over them and why you are so intent on thinking about them. Do you want revenge? If so, what purpose will that serve? Will it fix your brokenness? Throw away your list as a representation you are no longer going to dwell on what he did but instead look at yourself and ways to improve who you are. Look at the ways you sin every day—the bad thoughts, the compromising, the desire for revenge—and ask the Lord to heal your heart and give you a new outlook so you can move ahead.

Are you still trying to figure out who was wrong?

- Instead of focusing on who was wrong, focus on ways you should have or could have handled things differently. Every time the temptation to think of how "wrong" he was arrives, set your mind on ways you can improve and things you learned from the wrongs you committed.
- At this point, what difference does it make who was wrong? It didn't matter in the breakdown of the marriage, and it definitely doesn't matter now.

Do you look for ways to get revenge?

- We have all most likely known divorced people who have spent their entire lives looking for ways to get revenge. Yet we have to give our desire for revenge and justice over to the Lord. Vengeance is God's business (Romans 12:19). Remember what we said about drinking the poison of unforgiveness. Not only does it embitter your spirit but it also robs you of a future and of your energy. It is going to take every ounce of energy for you to build your new life and for you to care for your children and their hearts, so wasting it on someone who is now gone from your life is not worth it.
- As hard as it may seem, look for ways to think of something positive about your former husband, even if it is something little. Do what you can to focus on the positive instead of the negative. Despite the tragedy of your divorce, the triumph is yet to come.

Do you feel you have unhealthy boundaries with your ex?

- Are you still operating as if you are husband and wife even though you are divorced? Does he come over when he wants? Does he knock when he comes over? Does he expect you to respond immediately to whatever he needs or asks? Are you still afraid of him? These are some serious boundary issues you should consider and definitely discuss with a professional about how to handle them. It's easy to get divorced and yet have your ex expect things from you only a married person would expect.

Are you harboring resentment or bitterness?

• Are you focused on everything "he" does? Everything "he" says? Try to keep your thoughts focused on ways you can change and get better, and less on what he has done, did, or is doing.

Are you seeking out a relationship or new marriage to replace your ex?

• Do you find yourself looking for someone? Do you go into each date hoping he will be "the one"? We know how hard it is to fill the void you are currently feeling with the right things. This is why girlfriends who are healthy and further down the road than you in the healing process are so important. Spend time with your friends, and make sure you have plans when the kids are away. Otherwise it is easy to find yourself compromising.

Do you find yourself self-medicating or demonstrating extreme behavior?

• Are you self-medicating with shopping, food, alcohol, men, and distractions to keep you from facing the reality of your life? When we talk about "self-medicating," we are not referring to medication prescribed temporarily by your counselor for depression or anxiety. We are speaking of how you fill the longing, the hole in your heart, with unhealthy choices. At some point you will have to stop these destructive behaviors to begin the process of healing, and the sooner you rid yourself of the Band-Aids, the faster the healing process will begin. Anything other than the Lord will continue to add heart bruises, destruction, and most of all distraction from your future and from your children.

• When we are in a vulnerable state and dealing with overwhelming feelings of loss, we have found it's almost impossible for most women to stay completely on track. We are not suggesting you act as if nothing is wrong, but we are suggesting that the road back to a new you is not the road of destruction. Look for things to fill your time that are going to feed your soul and lift you up instead of take you further down into depression. Some things we suggest are feed the homeless, volunteer once a week at a community outreach, or take up a new hobby or sport. These are all things we have both seen women do that have not only helped them stay away from more destructive behaviors but have also helped in the healing of their hearts.

Do you feel stuck or in limbo?

- Baby steps, baby steps, baby steps will help you begin to move out of the fog and into the light. Every day, plan to do one thing to help you forge forward. It could be simply creating a new account in your name, or organizing a family dinner with you as the new head of the household. It's true, you are the new head of your household, and the kids are looking to you, and other people are looking to you.
- As hard as it is, be the leader and move forward. Day by day begin walking that out. It will get easier, and the longer you walk in your new shoes, the more you will begin to feel comfortable in them.

Do you look for ways to find out what your ex is doing, even if it means using the children?

- I know it is hard not to be curious about what he is doing, who he is seeing, if he is happy, if he's moved on more easily than you had hoped he would. These are normal curiosities, especially for those who didn't want the divorce. However, your kids are hurting, and the last thing you want to do is put them in the middle of the two of you. Set aside your desire to know these things in order to keep your kids from feeling more instability and having to make a choice between their mother and father. Their healthiness is dependent on you and your former spouse being able to continue to make them feel loved and not forcing them to choose sides.

YOU and Acceptance Prayer

Lord, help me accept the things I cannot change. Help me entrust to You the things that are unjust, unacceptable, and painful beyond words. Lord, help me let go of my past so I can begin the process of building a future. Help me know what boundaries to create, and give me the strength to implement them. Lord, help me focus on what is of good report and the ways I can become better and not bitter. In Jesus' name, amen.

two

YOU AND FORGIVENESS

If there were a chapter we would deem most important, it would be this chapter on forgiveness. It's the chapter we want you to pay attention to the most. Why? Because your freedom depends on it, your future depends on it, and your children's future depends on it. Forgiveness is critical to your emotional health and the emotional health of those you love most. As we said in the previous chapter, holding on to unforgiveness is like drinking deadly poison and hoping the other person dies from it.

The reason we find it hard to forgive is because we tend to feel justified in our minds, our hearts, and our spirits as to why we desire revenge and refuse to let go of the offenses against us. Focusing on injustices, real or not, keeps us rooted in deadly emotion, turning to anger, and enslaving us to our past. Surrendering the injustices and the outcome to God and forgiving those who have trespassed against us frees us and gives us a future. Let go of what you cannot control. God is a much better avenger. He will bring justice to all when we see Him face-to-face. Ask yourself, "How have I offended? Let me forgive so I may be forgiven."

Holding on to anger that eventually turns to bitterness is allowing a fortress to be built around your heart. Eventually you cannot get out, and no one can enter. Surrendering the outcome of your life to God and forgiving one another and your enemies keeps you alive and free. Why would you choose to live in prison and let your enemy run free? Forgiveness sets us free.

It's a new day, friends! Whatever is behind you, leave it. Those you haven't forgiven, forgive. Things you haven't let go of, let go. Grow from yesterday, live for today, and dream and plan for tomorrow. Don't get stuck in the past and let it keep you from your today and your future.

You may be thinking, *That all sounds so wonderful, it really does, but I can't get rid of this anger, this hate, this desire for revenge. It looms over me like an unwanted blanket and consumes my mind and heart daily.* You will experience a season of anger and even hate in some cases. It would be totally unreasonable to think you would come out of such a traumatic experience, with tremendous heart bruises received along the way, and get up and act as if all were fine. Your heart has been wounded. Your mind has been through an experience of loss and trauma. So moving ahead and out of the past experience is a process.

A LONG ROAD BACK

Michelle

I liken a divorce victim to someone who has experienced a major car accident. The victim was thrown through the windshield and left for dead on the road. There were passersby, but they could do nothing. There were even those with the victim who may have made it worse, or possibly even caused it. Regardless of the circumstances, the accident happened, the victim is in ICU, and she needs some time to recover. No one would ever expect the victim of a major car accident to get up and walk out of the hospital totally fine. Everyone would understand that it is going to be a long road back.

I have a dear friend who was hit by a car while he was riding his bicycle. When I got the call, I began to pray immediately. There were concerns as to whether he would survive. He made it through a long surgery where the doctors made the decision to remove part of his arm. This would be a horrifying situation for anyone, but it was even more devastating because my friend is a musician. My husband and I were deeply saddened by this news and have been there to support him in any way possible as he has begun the process of rehabilitation. He has to learn a whole new way of living with one arm. And this is only the physical ramification; there are also the emotional consequences. It will be a long road back.

Such is the case for the divorce victim. Don't have unrealistic expectations for yourself. You, too, will recover, but it will take a few months or, in most cases, a few years. This is a long process of healing and moving toward wholeness and restoration. You had surgery of the emotional kind, and what was removed, what was lost, was a way of life you have known maybe for many years. Even if you despised your former spouse, you still have to go through the process of recovery and loss from the marriage. People may expect you to recover immediately. They will begin setting you up with people and even encourage you to move on and get over it. This is likely because they have not experienced divorce, and they have no idea that while you may look fine on the outside, you are an ICU victim and need a lot of nurturing and comfort as well as the mercy and grace to heal with time and not be rushed into anything.

I personally have experienced all the above. It was not easy walking out the journey of healing with no one who really understood all that was happening, not even myself. I had no idea why I felt the way I did, why I couldn't get past the pain, the anger, the injustice. It was gut wrenching. I hated my former spouse for allowing our divorce, and I hated him for making me feel hate I had never had before. I was angry with God for not finding a way to stop it, and I shut Him out of my life for more than a year. Little did I realize I was shutting out my lifeline, my only hope.

I remember so well, as if it were yesterday, those dark days. I never thought my heart would change. I knew it had to change for my children's sake, but I didn't know the journey back. The Lord was faithful to me. He kept using people to reach me, to love me, to show me His amazing mercy. Looking back, it really is incredible the way He nurtured me back to health and how He used the most unlikely people to do so.

For instance, I'll never forget the passionate woman who came to my door one night when I was depressed. Emotionally and physically drained from the depressive state I was in and feeling unable to cook, I called and ordered pizza. The kids and I sat watching a movie while waiting for our food to be delivered. When the knock on the door came, all five of us went running, expecting it to be the delivery guy with our pizza.

When I opened the door, I was surprised to find it was not the pizza guy but a saleslady pitching magazines. She rambled on quickly before I even had a chance for the words "I am not interested" to come out of my mouth. She described this terrible dilemma that if she didn't sell enough magazines she would not win the big trip to Jamaica. Well, obviously being in my own more serious dilemma, I have to admit I didn't have a lot of compassion for her sad story. I blurted out how I was newly divorced and definitely not able to help her. As I began to close the door, this wonderful woman asked if she could pray for me. I couldn't believe my ears. I feebly agreed. I stepped out onto the porch, and this godly woman wrapped her strong arms around me and held me as she prayed. My kids gathered around and laid their little hands on my shoulders as they prayed along with her.

This woman belted out a prayer like you would not believe. I am sure everyone in the kingdom of heaven heard her pray. She prayed exactly what I needed her to pray, even down to details no one but I knew about. Tears in my eyes, I hugged her tight and thanked her from the bottom of my heart.

I'm convinced God sent her to show His love for me. My feet were not only stuck to the ground, but my face was there as well. I could not lift off and definitely was not having an eagle moment. If I wouldn't go to church, He would bring church to me. God proved over and over His love for me, even when I thought for sure He had left me. I knew I would never be able to do anything for Him again. This love, this amazing love we sing about and read about in His Word, captured my heart. Here I was, so undeserving, so ashamed of my current failure and every failure before—and once again, just as He had done when I came to know Him, He proved His unconditional love to me. I know we are told as believers we are not worthy except by the blood of Jesus, but it isn't really until you are in a place of crisis and feel stuck there that you completely recognize how true that statement is.

Somehow we think if we are doing all the right things as

Christians, then we are exempt in some way from the truth that only the blood of Jesus makes us righteous. No one is exempt. *We all desperately need God*, and acknowledging this is the first step to becoming a person crazy in love with God. Who wouldn't be crazy about Someone who loves us when we are the most unlovable, who loves us in the muck of it all, in our complete failure, or complete disappointment and shame? What would you not do for a person who treated you with such love and kindness? No human being can love you completely without condition. Every person at some point will fail you in some way. Only God has earned our loyalty; our focus belongs only on Him. When we are most concerned about an audience of One instead of an audience of many, we will meet our fullest potential. This is freedom, and this is where our Christian journey will finally become all it was intended to be.

What an obvious demonstration of God's tender heart for me. His love, His faithfulness, melted my heart back to a healthy place to receive love and give love again. Can you relate? Do you feel it seems impossible to love, to trust, to open up your heart? It's tough, and there is definitely a season of protecting your heart and guarding it until it's healthy enough to be vulnerable again. Enduring continuous heart bruises and pain will only hinder your healing process, not help it.

What are we holding on to? Who are we holding in contempt? If God has given us grace and forgiveness in the areas of our lives where we have failed, are we able then to extend that same grace and mercy to someone else? It is difficult to forgive when we feel justified, when we feel someone has wronged us and deserves to be punished. It's difficult to let the offense go, believing that to forgive him somehow means we are okay with what he did to us.

This is not the case. To forgive is our response to God, saying to Him, "I trust You to handle the situation the way You see fit. I trust You with the outcome of my life." What right do we have to make him pay? Is he hurt by us holding on to the offense? When we harbor unforgiveness in our hearts, are our offenders somehow paying for their sins?

I have met over and over again women who have not forgiven their former spouses. They have been divorced for years and are still wearing the blanket of bitterness all over their faces. Bitterness begins in the heart, but the evidence of it is eventually worn in our demeanor, our countenance. The longer we hold on to unforgiveness, the more bitter we become and the more our countenance reveals a hardness of heart. You may have met people like this: they spew out the injustices of their perpetrators as if to put them on trial over and over again in their minds—and they even express this bitterness in front of their children, who eventually begin to spew out the same offenses.

The sad part is, their former spouses still controls them. They are still tied to that person as long as they hold on to the bitterness. I met a couple who had been divorced, and they would say the most horrible words to one another every time they spoke. They would talk to each other with such a degrading tone and take pleasure in hurting each other. I counseled the woman to forgive him, and she began to take steps toward releasing the anger, the hurt, and letting go of this man who had wronged her. Today she and her ex are able to speak cordially and sometimes even nicely to each other. They have both softened and have moved on with their lives, but it took surrendering their control, their will, and their power to God in order for the change to take place. Are you holding your ex in contempt? Have you forgiven him? Do you have tormenting thoughts about how he has wronged you, done an injustice to you?

I have had to forgive a lot of offenses in my life. As a teenager I experienced date rape, and then later in life was raped again when someone forced his way into my house and attacked me. But I think the hardest thing I have ever had to let go of and release to the Lord was when I went through my divorce with my husband. Even years later, I continue to have to deal with the fallout of the marriage. If I had held on to the bitterness and anger, I'd be in a constant battle for the rest of my life. There are many times when I feel right, I feel my ex is definitely being impossible, and I evaluate, "Is the bitterness worth it? Can I let this go in order to keep the peace and work for the greater mission: our children?"

I did not want a divorce. There had been no divorce in my family, and I had witnessed my parents' marriage endure great trials and overcome. I felt sure the kids' father and I could do the same if we had both been willing, but this was not the outcome. I was devastated and felt angry not just with my then-husband, but also with God.

I knew eventually I would have to make the choice to take my eyes off what I *felt* had been done to me and focus on what I needed to change. I had to ask myself hard questions about the things I could have and should have done differently. None of us wants to look at our own responsibility when things go wrong. We want to shift the blame or stay in denial of our own sin, but this only hinders our growth in Christ and keeps us from intimate relationship with Him. If there is anything I have taught my kids, it is to take responsibility for their actions. Don't shift the blame or focus on what the other person has done without looking at what you could have done. It's never easy to look at what we have done or how we could have been better in our response. Looking back, of course, we always have answers. It's when we are in the midst of it all that we fall short.

If I had continued to allow hate and thoughts of anger to control my life, I would have been tormented by feelings of injustice, and those feelings would have eventually led to bitterness and hardness of heart. When our hearts are shut down due to unforgiveness, we also shut down our relationship with God. My feelings of anger and hate did not leave me right away. It was a determination and choice of my will. I had to submit myself to forgive my former husband while allowing the Holy Spirit to work in my heart and life. It was definitely not in my strength to forgive, but by the power of the Holy Spirit I was able to find victory.

God asks each of us, *Will you forgive those who have betrayed you, persecuted you, abused you, condemned you, shamed you, forgotten you, abandoned you?* My answer is, "Yes, Lord." I say yes. What do you say? I refused to forgive my ex for a time, but the more I focused on me and my sins and shortcomings, the less I was angry with him, and the easier I was able to forgive the offense.

During and after my divorce, memories surfaced of past relationships that had also wounded me. Have you found yourself not only dealing with the aftermath of the wounds your divorce left but also past wounds and memories? After my divorce I knew I had to deal with my hurt, my unforgiveness, and my unmet expectations. I even looked at the ways I may have provoked the anger and hurt in my former husband. Have you thought about the ways you wounded your former spouse?

Facing it head-on and dealing with the pain bring healing and the ability to forgive. For five years after my divorce, I continued to work through areas in my life I felt were unresolved. As the healing came, my anger left. It was not easy for me to forgive him or the others who had hurt me, nor was it easy to look at areas in which I could have responded in a better way; but I knew for my healing and my restoration, I had to do both.

My choice to forgive has allowed me to be able to work with my kids' father in their best interest. My forgiving him took down the walls he held up from his own hurt and wounds and set him free, enabling him to be more willing to work with me in everything to do with the kids. I have people tell me quite often how amazed they are at the relationship I have with my former spouse, the father of my four kids.

The goal is not about getting your former spouse to respond to you in a way that is agreeable. It could be the result, and most likely will be if you are kind and willing to work with him. However, forgiveness is an act of obedience that is based simply on the freedom Christ desires from you and not on the outcome of your obedience. You obey, and the results that follow are totally up to God and the heart of your former spouse. He may be impossible and still full of hate. It's not in your control. You control your heart and what you do, and the rest you surrender to God and entrust to Him to handle, and He will in time.

The peace God gave me after my divorce and the agreeable way in which my kids' dad and I work through their well-being would not have been possible if I would not have obeyed God's Word. I was left with a choice: to believe God's Word was true or not to believe. I knew I had to choose to lean on His understanding even though I felt justified to hate, justified not to forgive, justified to continue to hang on to all that had been done to me. I had to choose the cross over my pride. As hard as this choice was,

I knew as a believer, as a follower of Christ, there was no choice but one. For the sake of my children, for the sake of my relationship with Jesus, I had no other choice than to choose God's way over my way and allow Him to deal with the outcome of my life and my former spouse.

THE STRUGGLE TO FORGIVE

Connie

In my opinion, forgiveness is the single most difficult thing for most of us humans to accomplish. Yet it is the one thing we *must* do if we are going to move on with our lives, especially in the area of relationships.

When it comes to forgiveness, so much of it depends upon your personality and how you were raised. I was talking to a friend who was raised in a Sicilian, Italian household like I was. Let me say that I love my heritage, and I'm not saying that *all* Italians are this way but emotions were always flying all over the place in our house. My friend shared that when it comes to forgiving, he has a horrible time dealing with it. If he feels he is betrayed, he just says, "You're dead to me." Honestly, I get that. I heard it over and over again in my own family.

"But we are new creatures in Christ," you say. Yes, that's true. We have an insightful response from the apostle Paul. This is the man who wrote most of the New Testament and had the road to Damascus experience. Here's what he says in Romans 7:18–20: "For I know that good itself does not dwell in me, that is, in my sinful nature. For I have the desire to do what is good, but I cannot carry it out. For I do not do the good I want to do, but the evil I do not want to do—this I keep on doing. Now if I do what I do not want to do, it is no longer I who do it, but it is sin living in me that does it."

If the apostle Paul struggled with sin, is it a wonder we do? We are all different. And some of us handle situations better than others. We are humans who walk in the flesh in a fallen world. Thank you, Adam and Eve. So we must strive daily to walk in the Spirit. And even then we stumble and fall. But God is there to pick us up.

The Romans 7 passage rings true in my own life repeatedly. As I was going through the stages of grief after my divorce, I really got stuck in the anger stage. You have no idea how many fleeting thoughts I had about calling Uncle Vito from the Chicago family and having them put Fred out of commission for a week or so. I wasn't serious, but the thought did cross my mind, I confess. Maybe I watched *The Godfather* one too many times. This is a dangerous road because we're seeking revenge on our offenders. Remember that God is the ultimate judge. He says, "Never take your own revenge, beloved, but leave room for the wrath of God, for it is written, 'Vengeance is Mine, I will repay,' says the Lord" (Romans 12:19 NASB). Does that mean we wait and hope for God to do something awful to the one who hurt us? No! As a matter of fact, a test of true forgiveness is for us to pray that God lets them off the hook. Whoa! "Are you kidding me right now?" you ask. I'm afraid I'm not.

In all seriousness, the only way to get past the anger stage is to forgive. So I made the *decision* to forgive, knowing that I could only forgive by giving it to God over and over again. I thought I was doing a great job with it all, but sometimes I am surprised when those old feelings resurface. I don't have to see my ex and his wife very often because they live in another state where my children and grandchildren live. But I do have to see them at my grandchildren's birthday parties. So anytime I know I will see them, I get prayed up, determined that I'm going to be gracious—not overly friendly, just gracious—remembering that my children and everyone else know that I am a Christian, so I try to live up to that title as best I can.

And then—*bam!*—it happens. Someone says or does something that tears the scab off the wound. I bleed profusely and try to maintain my state of graciousness. And even if I make it, my feelings don't match my actions. I'm seething inside, thinking, *I can't believe he/she said/did that. What is he/she thinking?* That's why forgiveness is a choice. Remember, it is not an emotion. It's a choice. I believe that one day, after enough positive behavior techniques are put into place, and with God's grace, our feelings will match our decision to forgive. That's why I say it's a process.

If not dealt with, unforgiveness can lead to bitterness, and bitterness can lead to physical, emotional, and spiritual disease. True forgiveness washes away resentment. Unresolved resentment will destroy you. It will gnaw away at your life. Try to pray for the ones who have wronged you. That's honestly a tough one for me. But when you do, it releases you. My friend Jane will pray for her offender and then say, "God, please help me mean it."

The Word says, "For nothing will be impossible with God" (Luke 1:37 NASB). And "I can do all things through Him who strengthens me" (Philippians 4:13 NASB). And we know that He says, "For if you forgive other people when they sin against you, your heavenly Father will also forgive you. But if you do not forgive others their sins, your Father will not forgive your sins" (Matthew 6:14–15). If we don't forgive others, then He won't forgive us. Yikes! We have to do it. The choice we have to make is clear. God wouldn't ask us to do anything He wouldn't help us do. I highly recommend that you read the story of Joseph in the book of Genesis, chapters 37–45. It is truly the most beautiful story of forgiveness. In the end God worked out the situation for everyone's good. It is a beauty-for-ashes story. Joyce Meyer says, "If you want the beauty, you have to give up the ashes." I love that.

I think we get confused sometimes about what forgiving really means. Many of us think of forgiveness as a way of restoring a relationship, and sometimes that is the case, but not always. It doesn't mean you deny what really happened; it means you don't dwell on it and don't let it consume you.

To help me to get to the place of forgiveness, I had to understand what it is and what it isn't. One of the best books I've ever read on this topic is called *Total Forgiveness* by R. T. Kendall.[1] Here are a few things I've learned about forgiveness:

- Forgiveness doesn't mean you have to go to the person and say, "I forgive you" (unless he asks you to forgive him) and be all kissy-face about it and have breakfast, lunch, and dinner with him.
- Forgiveness isn't a feeling. It's a choice, an act of your will. For everyone, the time frame of arriving there is different. Just be willing to do it, and you'll eventually get there.
- Forgiveness is not pardoning the person who wronged you for what they did. A pardon releases the consequences of their actions. Instead, forgiveness is releasing them to God.
- Forgiveness doesn't keep a record of the wrong and bring it up over and over again. It is refusing to punish the

person who did wrong to you and leaving it in God's hands. Vindication is God's responsibility.

- Forgiveness is not forgetting what the offender has done. It is usually impossible to forget meaningful events in our lives. It is a demonstration of greater grace when we are fully aware of what happened, yet we still choose to forgive.

Some of Jesus' last words on the cross were, "Father, forgive them, for they do not know what they are doing" (Luke 23:34). Most of the time those who wronged you have no idea how deeply their actions have affected you. Maybe you've repented for something you did and you can't forgive yourself. Maybe you're angry with God because you've gotten involved with other people, trusting them with your heart because you thought they were "the one," and they broke your heart again. I confess; this happened to me—twice—all right, maybe three times since my divorce. It's okay. God can take it. The important thing is not to stay in that place.

In fact, allow me to embellish on a time in my life when I was furious with God. Immediately after my divorce, I began dating Brandon. Our relationship seemed to be long-lasting but then went belly-up. After my breakup with Brandon, I was so devastated that I thought the only way I could heal from that tragic episode was to have another man in my life. If I'd only listened to the advice of DivorceCare and just cooled my jets in the man department, my healing would've come much sooner. Oh well, better late than never.

I remember going into the chapel at church with a list I'd composed containing the attributes of the perfect guy for me and kneeling before God, begging Him to send me the right man—and please let it be this year. Ha! I shake my head when I think of this. What kind of prayer was that for a mature believer in the Lord? As if God needed me to make Him a list and tell Him when to deliver! I also asked the Lord to reveal to the man that I was the woman for him. Kind of like the story in the Bible where Abraham's servant was out looking for a wife for Isaac (Genesis 24). He prays for success that day and asks that the first woman who shows up and offers him a drink and water for his camels will be the one the Lord has chosen. Sure enough, a little while later, Rebekah comes to the well saying the exact thing Abraham's servant prayed for. Well, my prayer was answered the same way . . . or so I thought.

A few months later, I was introduced to a man named James at a party through a trusted friend. I was intrigued but not really attracted to him. I began talking to him on the phone. He had a great sense of humor, and I loved his voice. He was into the same music I was into, and we were having wonderful conversations about the Lord. I decided to go to dinner with him, and that evening he sat with tears in his eyes and told me everything I wanted to hear. Then he topped it all off with, "And God told me that you are the woman for me." Well, my heart leaped because that was specifically what I had prayed for.

This man pursued me with a vengeance. We women love to be pursued because that's the way it's supposed to be. He was captivated by me, enthralled. So I gave him my heart. His family thanked me for bringing a smile back to James's face. And I had been thanking God for bringing me into James's life. About three months later, he wasn't calling anymore and started fading out of my life. He finally admitted that he met another girl at the gym, and I was history. I was devastated again! And I was mad at God for bringing that man into my life who seemed to answer my specific prayer to Him. This guy was the counterfeit guy. This guy was definitely a wolf in sheep's clothing. I hate it when they wear that outfit, and I fail to see the gaps in the costume. How could God do this to me? I couldn't even pray for a while, I was so mad.

Well, here's the rest of the story. James was separated but was not legally divorced yet. So, in all truthfulness, I was seeing a married man. I make this admission because I don't want you to make the same mistake I did. Wait until the person is free and has had a chance to go through some healing. Would God tell a man who wasn't totally free from his wife that I was the woman for him? That's not how God operates. Everything God would say has to line up with His Word, and the timing of this one was all wrong. It was my own fault for dating this guy too soon and trusting him with my heart. In the end, I had to forgive James, I had to forgive myself, and I had to ask God to forgive me. God got over it, and so did I. God and I are on great terms now.

What I've learned over the last ten years, through my own story, is that to get to the place of true healing, the place where you're ready to move on, you have to get to the place of acceptance. To get to the place of acceptance, you must walk the road of forgiveness. Acceptance is your destination. It is surrendering to what is and moving on. God wants us to be in a place of complete surrender to Him. And in that place we find total peace—the peace that surpasses all understanding. The bottom line is this: if you want to live your life to the full intent, purpose, and potential and reap the harvest of blessings He has for you, then you must forgive. Honestly, if this little Italian firecracker can do it, so can you.

YOU and Forgiveness Thoughts

The Beatles sang the song "Let It Be." Our song for this chapter is "Let It Go." Take off the weight of the monster of unforgiveness. Be free and let it go.

In all our years of therapy, a wise counselor told us six words that were gold: "Just do the next right thing." Boy, do we wish we would've listened to that advice a time or two.

Every day is filled with decisions. And some of the decisions you make today will affect your life twenty years from now. If you decide to soak in the sun every day all summer long and don't cover your face, twenty years from now your face will look like a leather road map. You can't see the damage it's doing to you now because it's underneath your skin. It is the same with forgiveness. Today you have the choice to forgive or to hold on to the anger and bitterness that is eating you alive. You can't see the damage it is doing to your heart today, but twenty years from now you will be a much older person who hasn't moved on. You're stuck. And the longer you hold on to it, the harder it gets. For today, tomorrow, the next day, and beyond, choose the right *F* word: *forgive*.

Initially, forgiving may be a choice we make mentally and not a decision of the heart, but eventually the heart will follow when it is healed and ready to do so. This is a process for some, and instantaneous for others. Every person is different. To live in denial and pretend we are not angry is as harmful as the anger itself. It's important to admit and face how you feel and be honest about it. God sees your heart, and exposing your feelings helps you heal. Sometimes you just need to yell out loud about how unfair the divorce is or how you still can't stand him. We are with you. We've been there and most certainly had our screaming moments, or what I would call crying out to God.

What are some of the ways you are still hanging on to unforgiveness? What are some of the ways you have justified it?

- *I have the right to be angry.* We are justified because our expectations were not met. God is a loving God. His ways are not our ways. We may not understand why, or what, but we do know He is a God who will vindicate us; He is our advocate, and we can entrust to Him even our anger. We will face trials and disappointments, but God has promised He will never leave us or forsake us, and if He is for us, who can ever be against us?

- *By holding on to the anger and hate, I am getting my former spouse back.* Holding on to your anger is not hurting your former spouse. If anything, it is satisfying to him to see he still has control over your emotions. Yep, as long as you hold him in contempt, you are tied to him. When you forgive, when you let him go, you can move on from the relationship and find your freedom. As long as you hold on to the anger, he has control over you, and your emotions are deeply impacted, depleting your energy.

- *Not forgiving him will change the situation and make him pay.* Holding on to resentment toward your former spouse doesn't change what has happened or the wrong that has occurred; instead, it worsens it and changes you. If we allow the root of anger and unforgiveness to remain in our hearts, then we are not able to receive forgiveness from God. Unforgiveness hardens our hearts and becomes an obstacle between us and God. "They are darkened in their understanding and separated from the life of God because of the ignorance that is in them due to the hardening of their hearts" (Ephesians 4:18).

- *I am justified in being angry toward this person.* As believers there are absolutely no reasons that justify remaining in anger toward another person. Jesus instructs us to love even our enemies and bless those who persecute us. This makes no sense to the world, but to a believer it is the only way we can continue to walk free of bitterness. Jesus said, "But I say to you that everyone who is angry with his brother shall be guilty before the court; and whoever says to his brother, 'You good-for-nothing,' shall be guilty before the supreme court; and whoever says, 'You fool,' shall be guilty *enough to go* into the fiery hell" (Matthew 5:22 NASB).

YOU and Forgiveness Actions

- Make the choice to forgive. Do it every day. It's a process. It's never easy to forgive someone who has wronged you, especially if you feel justified. Continue to ask the Lord to help your heart soften in this area.

- Think about all the times God has forgiven you when you don't deserve it. Actually take a moment and think through things you have done wrong in life and did not deserve grace. How great is the forgiveness and mercy God has shown you? Who are we not to give this same grace to someone else who in our eyes could even be undeserving?

- If you must, get into an anger management class or grief counseling. Sometimes processing your feelings with someone else is helpful to the forgiveness process.

- If you really want to get on with your life in a healthy, productive way, begin to "Let It Go." Remember who you are hurting. You are hurting yourself and the kids the longer you hold on to the bitterness. Sometimes letting go is easier knowing you are benefiting as well.

- Remember, Jesus said if we don't forgive those who've sinned against us, He will not forgive us our sins. So realize that unforgiveness creates a barrier to getting your prayers answered—because we are holding on to sin, resentment, and anger. God forbid!

Let Go of Past Regret and Failure

Release the disappointment of your divorce to the Lord. In your prayer time ask the Lord to begin healing the memories and to begin showing you how to be free of the guilt your divorce may have brought with it. Write down ways you have grown as a result of your divorce, in your spiritual life as well as your emotional life. Bitter or better is always the question, and even if you have chosen bitter in the past, it's time to choose to get better. It is never too late.

Recognize the Anger Is Real

When people hurt you, betray you, or you feel disappointed in life, you cannot pretend not to be angry. As Christians it's easy to think, *I can't be angry because I am a Christian.* It's unrealistic to not feel anger when people hurt you and especially in the case of a divorce. We are not superhuman, and God never said you are never to be angry. He said not to sin during your anger. Acknowledge you are angry, and allow God to begin a work in your heart. He will heal the pain if you open yourself up to being set free. Every day spend time in worship, allowing it to soften your heart. It's hard to keep a hardened heart when you listen to worship music. It works to open your heart back up to God so the healing can begin. Also, reading the Word is imperative. The Word is convicting and full of power that will help you do what you need to do as it relates to forgiving.

Repent

I know some of us have not-so-good memories of a preacher pointing at us from the pulpit and shouting, "Repent!" Repentance is not a sign of God's anger; it's a sign of God's love. He loves us so much and wants us to walk in pureness with Him. In order to do so, we must repent of our sin before Him and ask His forgiveness so we will be forgiven. When we repent of our sin, God is then able to begin the healing. Allow God to begin the healing in you. Repent and ask Him to forgive you.

Forgive Your Offender

Forgive, forgive, forgive, seventy times seven, God said. Why do you think He said to forgive seventy times seven? Jewish tradition called for God's people to forgive three times, so when Jesus responded for them to forgive seventy times seven, He was saying to them their forgiveness should be unending. We must extend forgiveness to our former spouses and those who hurt us in the divorce over and over again, the same way we expect to go to Christ over and over again when we sin. There have been a couple of times when I just didn't know how I could ever forgive what was done to me. In those moments, I would concentrate on the ugliness of my own sin in order to forgive the one who wronged me. This helped me have mercy and compassion for the other person, and I was able to forgive that person in time.

Pray

When you pray, God helps you release to Him your former spouse and the hurt he caused you. Lay it at the altar, and ask God to help you in your journey to overcoming. Ask the Lord to begin to heal the memories that stay in your mind and are reminders of why you can't forgive him. God is faithful to those who want to pursue healing. He is the healer of our emotions and our physical ailments.

YOU and Forgiveness Prayer

Lord, forgive me. Forgive me for sinning in my anger against my former spouse. I cry out to You for mercy. Please renew my mind, erase the bad memories, and transform my heart. Peel away the layers of hardness that have built up through the sin of my bitterness and unforgiveness. Lord, please strengthen me and help me forgive him and others who have wounded me. Forgive me for wounding him and others in my anger.

Lord, help me lean on You for wisdom and not lean on my own understanding. Help me be slow to speak to him and to my children regarding him, and be slow to anger and not sin when I am angry. Thank You for delivering me from this anguish and torment that rages in my soul. I need Your living water to flow through me again.

Holy Spirit, replenish me, and cause love to pour through me once again. Free me from my guilt and disappointment. Free me from everything keeping me from my purpose and the wholeness You desire for me. In Jesus' name, amen.

three

YOU AND BEING ALONE

Loneliness can cause you to do crazy things, so it's important to get to the place where you are comfortable with aloneness. Aloneness doesn't have to equal loneliness. It's becoming okay with being alone and accepting that aloneness is not a bad thing. This is easier said than done. There are some women who, after divorce, are able to adjust to the idea of being alone and may not experience the feeling of being lonely. For those of you who feel tremendous despair when it comes to learning to be alone again, this chapter is for you. We can both relate. We didn't even want to write this book alone! Aloneness is something we are very familiar with having to adjust to and live with; it is a process.

We love that scene in *Hope Floats* where Harry Connick Jr.'s character, Justin Matisse, is sitting at a table alone in a restaurant and says to Sandra Bullock's character, Birdee, "You have to look like you chose to be alone, seem mysterious." So funny and so difficult to do right after a divorce when the last thing you want to do is be alone.

Working through being alone and feeling comfortable with

it is a part of your journey to a happy, healthy life. You have to experience wholeness before being alone will be something you are comfortable with. You can do it. It may seem impossible right now, but you will get there, and we are here to walk with you and let you know you are not alone, even though you may feel very alone right now.

You may do everything possible to avoid being alone, even if it means being in a relationship with a man who is undesirable or unhealthy for you. Moments without the kids can be the worst. Your ex may have the kids, or if you don't have kids, everyone you know is married and out with their families. Doing things by yourself, or sleeping alone at night, is likely not high on your list of desirables, but when you make decisions out of those feelings, your choices will further damage you emotionally and cause more heart bruises. To go out with someone just to avoid being alone, or to have a sexual relationship with someone just so you can feel someone close, will not help you; it will hinder and prolong something so much greater that God wants to do in you and through you. So take a deep breath, and let's talk about this some more.

There are moments when the sound of silence seems unbearable, the empty side of the bed next to you seems miserable, or sitting down to dinner with no one to talk to can seem absolutely depressing, but there is hope. You may never totally get used to these alone moments, but you can get to the place where you are comfortable with them. Some single women get so comfortable being alone that it's hard for them to adjust when they do meet someone.

So let's discuss ways to walk in the confidence needed to see yourself not as a poor, rejected soul with no friends or opportunity, but instead as a woman of confidence who has chosen to get out and experience life and is not afraid to meet new people or enjoy the sound of her own thoughts and opinions on life, while enjoying dinner alone. Do you think you can get there? We hope to encourage you to do so.

BUILDING COMMUNITY AND FAMILY

Michelle

When you are no longer married, it's easy to feel like you are going to have to wait until you are married to feel whole again. Not true. You are basically having to build a new life, and this new life will look different. I walked around for years feeling like part of me was missing and thinking I needed a new husband to come into my life for me to feel whole. I wish I would have understood how to create community when I first divorced.

I did immediately put mentors and people around my kids who would have an effect on them both spiritually and emotionally, who would affirm my beliefs, and who would be great role models for them. Since my boys' dad was not there all the time, I wanted men around them who would be great leaders and would help shape them. I am thankful for them. I also had awesome women who were role models for my daughter, teaching her to value herself and believe she was made for greatness. Kids need to be affirmed, especially kids from divorced households. It's important to fill those gaps that are missing as a result of the household dividing. I would purposely get my children around people with great marriages—not perfect marriages, but great ones. I wanted my kids to know that marriage is not a bad thing, and there were many marriages that were good and healthy.

My decision to create community, allowing others to be a part of my kids' lives, was intentional. It's easy because of our woundedness and pain to do the opposite—to shelter, protect, and build up an us-against-the-world mentality, becoming isolated from the community we need to survive. I refused to allow my kids to be victims or feel like they suddenly were "different" just because they didn't have a two-parent household. While we are victims of divorce, we are not victims for life, and our identities are not based in divorce. It doesn't define who we are, nor does it define our children if we don't allow it.

When I was first divorced, my kids chose to hang around other kids whose parents had divorced. I remember the kids saying to me, "They understand, Mom, because their parents are divorced." But I didn't want them to choose friends based on whether their parents were divorced. I wanted them to see healthy marriages being modeled and encouraged them to also seek out friends who had parents with good marriages as well. I knew this was how they dealt with it at first. It was easier to be with friends who could relate to their experience, but I didn't want them to choose friends for that reason only. I am thankful over time they didn't feel it was an issue or a reason for choosing. In fact, now as young adults they work to find role models who can model what a healthy marriage looks like.

I also have brothers and sisters who have modeled healthy marriages. Just because we are products of a divorce doesn't mean our children have to be if we are open to being honest about it and allowing the support necessary. It would be easy for our kids to become cynical toward marriage. I tell my kids all the time, "Marriage is not broken; people are broken, but marriage is not broken." God designed marriage to be a beautiful covenant.

Once I realized how to be vulnerable to people and ask for help and let people know I was struggling in areas, I began to get the support I needed to live a healthy life. It doesn't have to be all about survival. With people around you whom you can call to help you with the daily maintenance of your home, carpooling, and the extras you need but can't afford, you will feel more like you are thriving instead of surviving. Singleness, or single parenthood, will still be a challenge, but it doesn't have to be a constant burden for you to bear alone. God never intended for us to do life alone.

Loneliness is often a result of our pride making us unwilling to say what we need. I have always been a strong person who could find a way to make it on my own. I was on my own in many ways at the age of sixteen. But for several years after my divorce, I fought to survive and keep my head above water. Financially I was okay, but I was doing everything myself . . . everything! It was so taxing, and I was exhausted all the time.

I began to build community out of sheer necessity, and it was in doing so that I began to find a new life. I found new friends who had also gone through divorce and could be a support to me. I found "safe" guys who were willing, with no strings attached, to help me around the house in exchange for a meal. I even began to spend my alone weekends doing something productive and planning something that would help me grow spiritually or that would be fun and give me something to look forward to.

I found the hardest moments were always, always, always when the kids were in bed, the house was quiet, and I was left to face the reality of my life with an empty bed and no one to discuss my day with. So I would get on the phone and talk to a friend until I was so exhausted I would have to go to sleep. However, as much as I did to make those moments easier, I will say they never went away completely. The busyness of the day would shelter me from loneliness, but when nightfall came, I was alone, and it was agonizing for the most part. Some nights were better than others.

So what changed? How can I expect you to deal with the loneliness when it sounds as if I couldn't? I would love to give you a formula, an answer to the question of how to survive the lonely nights. How do I get used to being alone, and how do I fill the empty feelings inside me? There is no formula, but what I found is the more I surrendered to the process, accepted where I was at the time, and allowed God to work in my heart and life, the easier it was for me to feel peace in my situation. I liken it to a desert place. I was in the desert, and what is worse than being in the desert is being in the desert alone. But I found I wasn't alone. I met Jesus there. When I began finding happiness in my desert place, when I began to look for all the wonderful ways to allow the desert to change me and make me better, when I began to find there was in fact water in the desert if I looked for it, I began to find joy in the midst of my trial, and no longer was I looking for counterfeits to fill the void. I wasn't looking any longer, period. Amazing!

I began to realize that the deeper my dependence and intimacy went in my relationship with Christ, the more peace and wholeness I felt. This wholeness gave me such confidence. It felt great to walk in complete certainty knowing my life, my loneliness, my aloneness, were in His hands, and He would change my situation if it was a part of my purpose and His plan for my life. I'm happy today to say it was. I love my husband and am grateful every night to be able to have someone so wonderful beside me, but Michael was an added, unexpected bonus who came after I had come to the place of accepting I might be single for life.

It's easy to make decisions based on your loneliness, but don't do it. Set your standards high on how you spend your time, and protect the time you have with your kids. Your responsibility is to them over anyone or anything. You want to make sure you aren't feeding your longings and forgetting theirs, so essential to their emotional health. I know it feels at times your emotional health is hard enough to take care of, but as a parent it's important you set aside your needs for theirs. You will be glad you did in the future, and people around you will respect you for it. Until someone becomes that special someone, you have to protect your relationship with your children.

Filling your longings doesn't always have to be about a person or sexual gratification. It could be you are self-medicating your pain with alcohol, drugs, or even shopping. I've seen people try to satisfy their needs with material things, especially right after the divorce. Any counselor or program for divorced people will encourage you not to make any big decisions for a while. You want those kinds of decisions to be well thought out and not based on some emotional whim. Again, when we have come to the place of total surrender and begin to lean on the Rock of our faith instead of filling ourselves up with counterfeits, we begin to walk in the peace and confidence that allows us to feel whole and complete. Loneliness will become less about agony and more about finding normalcy and peace; and aloneness will feel less embarrassing and about rejection and more about feeling comfortable with where you are. If you can get to this place before you meet someone, you can have a much more rewarding relationship. And you will find yourself evaluating the new someone and seeing where he is in his journey. It is just as important he has found his wholeness in Christ and isn't seeking you to fill a void in his own life.

So what does wholeness really mean? We know until we see Christ face-to-face we will not experience true wholeness, but while we are on this earth, it's important for us to find any wholeness we are looking for in our relationship with Christ. What does that look like?

The gaping hole that plagues most people in their search for significance is something many have wondered about, longed to fulfill, and traveled the world to find. You don't have to be divorced to be searching to fill this "holeness." It just seems to become more apparent when you are divorced. All of a sudden the hole seems to be caused by your loss, but in reality it has been there, and you were filling it with other counterfeits. In our despair we find ourselves desiring and longing for wholeness because there are no longer distractions to keep us unaware of the void. Now that we have more than enough alone time, we find ourselves with heightened senses to everything in our lives. This includes our spiritual bankruptcy. There is nothing like pain to cause us to go deeper with God. It's a known fact, and its evidence is seen throughout God's Word. Even the Israelites, when blessed and in a time of abundance, forgot their Maker and turned instead to other gods and counterfeit loves.

We make choices, and it's in those choices we get responses. Which choice will you make: the counterfeit or the real solution? Jesus is the answer to all our longings and need for affirmation and love. He truly is, but most of us have to go around the block a few times, and then a few times more, before realizing this truth.

Our hope is that you will take our word for it and that we are able to save you some heartache and more pain.

In our desire to find wholeness again, it's easy to see why so many divorcées reach for the wrong things. Second, third, and fourth marriages are common among the divorced, and unfortunately it's a consequence of our desire to fill the hole and ease the pain. The void left in your heart from a broken marriage can be agonizing and debilitating; you may feel lost and confused, and it's easy in this place to make wrong choices.

I did.

I'd love to share with you how perfectly I walked out my post-divorce life. With no one to help me navigate the waters, I learned by trial and error, which is never any fun.

My divorce wasn't even final when well-intentioned friends suggested I get out there and begin testing the waters with their friends. I was so broken; I didn't have the sense to know any better. All I knew was I needed and longed for someone to hold me, help me, protect me, and save me. I felt like I was drowning. Everywhere I went people assumed I was fine, yet I was doing everything I could to simply keep my head above the water. As a mother, I also was thinking of my four children and how I would raise them without a man in my life, without the income we once had. In fact, all I could think of was, *How would I do anything without a man in my life?* These are good questions many of us ask. The problem for me is I had no one to ask for answers. I knew not one divorced couple. I never had imagined myself divorced. It seemed like I was living someone else's life, not my own.

When you have no one to help you navigate, to help you steer the wheel in the right direction, it's very easy to get off course. I hope we are helping you navigate. It's our hearts.

There are predators who are intentionally looking for women who are vulnerable to take advantage of them. You have heard the term *rebound*. Why do we rebound? We rebound because we are not stable enough to make good, wise decisions, and we therefore find the first person who gives us attention and makes us feel amazing. A man cannot heal you, he cannot save you, and he cannot keep you safe. No one but Jesus Himself can do this for you.

One day you wake up and realize you've made a mistake. You aren't anywhere near ready to be in a relationship, much less discern a life partner. That is where I was. Weak and beaten down, I was not in a place to make wise choices. Can you relate? Do you feel worn down? Setting up the proper boundaries right after a divorce is so important.

When well-meaning people would say to me, "God will be your husband," I would get angry. I'd think, *You can say that because you are married*. However, God *can* be your husband. He can be your everything, and once He is, you will feel healthy and whole. When we are needy, desperate, and in need of healing, it's easy to find commonalities with someone in the same place. This can be a dangerous thing. It is almost impossible for two people who are both in an unhealthy place to build something healthy.

When you are healthy and whole, when you feel strong and know your value again, and if it is meant to be and is God's will for your life, you will attract someone who is also healthy and whole. You can't build a marriage on sinking sand. When God brought me Michael, I had become comfortable with being single. I was finally feeling whole and emotionally healthy. I would walk into a room and no longer feel as though there was an arm missing or a hole in my chest revealing the loss in life. I had worked through it all and fought hard to become strong again.

I did the hard work week after week in the counselor's office. I was focused on working through the things *I* needed to change, heal from, and fight to overcome. I had a lot of destructive thinking I needed to rid myself of. I pressed in for my healing and was determined to get healthy again. After my divorce, I felt like someone had beaten me up and thrown me over the ledge of the Grand Canyon. I had a long climb back to the top, but Jesus was with me every step of the way. I'd climb a few steps, then fall back down, climb a few steps more, and fall back down again. It was never perfect, but my heart wanted to get back to the right place again, to pursue my emotional and spiritual health. What is your heart telling you? Are you ready to be back emotionally and spiritually?

I've heard people say marriage is broken. I disagree. Marriage is a beautiful thing. People are broken. If two people won't fight for their marriage, won't believe and trust their souls to each other, leaving God at the center instead of being each other's center, they won't make it.

Your aloneness and my aloneness are in God's hands. Because of Him, ultimately we are never alone, and whether you desire to marry again or date again, it's important to have a healthy outlook on marriage itself.

DANCING WITH JESUS

Connie

For a woman who is by nature an extrovert, a social butterfly, a people person, I spend an enormous amount of time alone. It has been a real test for me to learn how to be comfortable with it. In all honesty, I'm not completely comfortable being single, but I'm dealing with it as best I can. I'm not married, and my kids are grown and gone.

As a voice-over artist and writer, I work alone. I get up in the morning and have my quiet time. Most of my day is quiet. I don't watch much television. So if I'm not on the phone, having people over, or listening to music, then it's pretty quiet around here. If I don't have a reason to get out, there are days I stay in my pajamas, drinking a cup of coffee and talking into a microphone or typing on a computer. And believe me, I love this. The flexibility I have with my job is a major blessing. But there's a lot of discipline that goes along with being self-employed. When I exercise, which I try to do most days, I don't go to a gym; I prefer to be outdoors, walking or cycling. Sometimes I walk with a friend and other times I'm alone. I hate to admit it, but I hardly know any of my neighbors because I live in a transient neighborhood and people are moving in and out all the time. I have my buddies, girlfriends I do things with regularly. For me, this "alone" thing is my new normal. I eat alone, sleep alone, travel alone, and work alone. Sounds kind of sad. So what's a girl like me to do? Build the Con-Vent, right?

Many people are dealing with the same kind of lifestyle I have, and they choose different things to fill in the gaps of their alone time. Most of the time it's social media or Internet dating, which we'll cover in the next chapter. The Internet is good and it's bad. There's an upside and a downside to most things in life. We just have to figure out where to draw the line and stay on the good side of it. Because of the Internet, I find that I've never spoken to most of my clients. The majority of my business is conducted through e-mail. This is a plus because I can communicate with more people quicker than making phone calls, but the downside is that I don't have personal one-on-one connections with them.

Some of us will try to stay busy and make lists of things to do to keep from feeling lonely. Some of us get wrapped up in reality TV shows and involved in other people's lives because we don't like being alone. Some of us look for love in the wrong places.

After all, the Word tells us in Genesis that it is not good for man to be alone. And I believe in the context of this chapter that God was referring to a man and a woman in a marriage sense and having a helpmate. I found an interesting fact when reading a book called *The Blue Zones* by Dan Buettner published by *National Geographic*.[1] In the book, Dan visits the four regions in the world where there is a large population of centenarians. And they were thriving centenarians who have a good quality of life. There were commonalities among all four of the regions. One of them was that there was a strong sense of family and/or community in their lives. Many of them lived with family members. Bottom line: they did not live alone. Studies are out now showing that married people typically live longer than single people. That's hard for me to believe since so many marriages are just hanging by a thread, but apparently there's something positive about having a living, breathing person around to do life with.

There's a big difference between being alone and being lonely. I am not lonely. And here is why: I have an abundance of wonderful friends in my life. Good relationships keep me from being lonely. I have many solid women in my life I can laugh with, pray with, cry with, and call on anytime. And they know they can call me and count on me to lend an ear, grab a coffee or dinner, have some good conversations, and bounce things off of. It's community. I have friends I get with one-on-one, and then there are groups of us that meet monthly. There are other ways to keep from being alone: getting involved in your local church, doing a hobby that you love, taking a class, joining a Bible study or a book club, or volunteering somewhere to help others. Some people say that having a pet helps them not to feel so alone.

The sad thing is that I know many people who are married, have great jobs, coworkers, and families—and they still feel lonely. Why? Here's the answer: the only thing that will truly fill the void inside you to keep you from feeling lonely is a relationship with your Creator. This is what our soul longs for—relationship with God. I can go to a beautiful park, walk alone, and commune with God in such a way that I know I'm not alone. Now that's rich. We're never alone.

This all came into perfect focus for me in August 2010. I had a cold that turned into laryngitis. It wasn't getting better after a week, so I went to the voice doctor. After looking at my vocal cords, he determined that my right vocal cord had ruptured. I had to be on complete vocal rest for about a month. I was devastated. Doing voice-overs and recording audios is how I generate most of my income. No talk, no moola. Yikes! So this girl now had to shut up for a month. I was determined that I was going to live my life as normally as possible and do all the things I always did, except without talking. So I walked around with a dry-erase board and marker and wrote everything down. I'd write people notes on my board and they'd write back. I wore a little button that said, "I'm on vocal rest; therefore, I'm unable to speak." People were so nice to me. They were treating me like I was handicapped . . . which I was, I guess. People would gesture back to me or mouth words at me with no sound because they thought I couldn't hear. I'd mouth back to them, "I can hear you." It was kind of funny, really.

But during this time I never felt alone. I felt the peace and presence of God in a much stronger way. My prayers were prayers of silence. Then, because I couldn't speak, I'd take the time to listen . . . a lot. It's amazing how when we take time off with our mouths, we become much better listeners. It's so important. Sometimes, when the mail would come with a bill that would be due, I'd be a little fearful about the fact that I wasn't earning one dime. I even wondered what I'd do if my voice didn't return the way it was and what I'd do if I had to look for a new career not involving the use of my voice. So one night I silently prayed about all my concerns before going to sleep, and the Lord gave me the most incredible dream that addressed all of them.

In the dream, I was dancing with Jesus. I didn't see His face, but I knew it was His. I saw the long white robe and long hair—the way most of us picture Him. It was truly the most romantic experience ever, in a pure sense. All I know is that I never wanted the dance to end. In the dance, He was holding me securely. I felt so safe. No one could harm me in His arms. He was showing me that He is my husband and protector. "For your Maker is your husband—the LORD Almighty is His name—the Holy One of Israel is your Redeemer" (Isaiah 54:5). He showed me that I am secure in His arms. He is my provider. "Therefore I tell you, do not worry about your life, what you will eat; or about your body, what you will wear. . . . Consider the ravens: They do not sow or reap, they have no storeroom or barn; yet God feeds them. And how much more valuable you are than birds" (Luke 12:22, 24).

In the dance, He was showing me a love that is endless and unconditional. "I am convinced that neither death nor life, neither angels nor demons, neither the present nor the future, nor any powers, neither height nor depth, nor anything else in all creation, will be able to separate us from the love of God that is in Christ Jesus our Lord" (Romans 8:38–39).

He showed me that He is committed to our relationship and is always there for me. I am in covenant with Him. "Never will I leave you; never will I forsake you" (Hebrews 13:5). *Never!*

And in the dance, He was leading me. He was ordering my steps and setting me on the right path. "The steps of a good man are ordered by the LORD, and He delights in his way" (Psalm 37:23 NKJV). "In all your ways acknowledge Him, and He shall direct your paths" (Proverbs 3:6 NKJV).

In the dream, I pulled back to look at His face, and I exclaimed, "Jesus! My voice is back, and it sounds so beautiful." He said, "Your voice is always beautiful when you praise Me." I woke up worshipping the Lord, of course in silence, for giving me this incredible dream. How sweet of Him to address every issue that concerned me and all the things I prayed about. This was what I call a kiss from God. I believe this dream wasn't just for me but for you as well.

YOU and Being Alone Thoughts

Today you may be alone, but you do not need to be lonely. You have a God who longs to commune with you and speaks to you daily if you will take time to listen. He is there—holding you, protecting you, providing for you, loving you, committed to you, and leading you. Carve out the life you want for yourself with work, family, friends, church, and so on—but *first* take time to do life with the One who created you. The One who is concerned about everything that concerns you.

In Him, there is fullness of joy. He truly is your everything, and the wholeness you long for is found within a relationship of abiding with Him and walking with Him. Meditating on all the wrong things only delays your healing and keeps you in a place of bondage.

We so desire to see you spiritually and emotionally healthy again. Not only are we here to walk through this with you, but God Himself loves you deeply and is longing for you to run into His arms every time your heart hurts. Every time you feel you cannot go on, seek Him and He will find you.

YOU and Being Alone Actions

- Begin to practice doing things alone and seeing it as something positive. Start with doing things where a lot of other people are present, like seeing a movie or sitting in a crowded coffee shop and reading a book. The goal is to eventually get to the place where you can go to dinner alone, be comfortable, and focus less on your past and more on your new future.
- When you feel desperately lonely, when you feel you cannot stand the silence, reach for the Bible instead of the phone or the computer. Listen to worship music, and spend some time praying. You'll be amazed at how it will change your heart and how less alone you will feel.
- One of the best ways to take your mind off yourself is to put your mind on others. Donate your time and talent to a cause or church. There is nothing more

healing than helping those who are in worse conditions than yourself.

- Begin to look for community and build it. Getting involved in a Bible study, particularly one that breaks into small groups, will help you get to know like-minded women. This takes time. You want to find safe people who will understand you and empathize with you, not those who will condemn or judge you.
- Rediscover yourself and all the things you love to do. Take a cooking class, or try something entirely new, like painting or pottery. Learn to play the piano or another instrument. If you have kids who go to their dad's house, have a plan in place during his possession periods so you don't find yourself with too much time to think and feel sorry for your situation.

YOU and Being Alone Prayer

Lord, my heart is hurting. There are times when I feel so lonely, so abandoned and lost. Please meet me in this desert place. Bring me people who will relate to where I am and will help me walk through this difficult time. Lord, help my heart heal and set me on a path to emotional and spiritual health. I desire to be whole, not to try to fill my void with the wrong things. But sometimes I feel weak. Lord, give me strength in these moments of weakness. Jesus, become my everything. You seem so far away, but I know You can become even more real to me than ever before. I need You so much right now. Give me wisdom to make the right decisions, and when I fall, when I have days where climbing to the next step seems impossible, help me get back up again so I can keep moving toward the wholeness You desire for me. In Jesus' name, amen.

four

YOU AND DATING

et's face it, girls. Dating isn't what it used to be. We got all dolled up, went out with our girlfriends—whether it was to a dance, restaurant, coffee shop, party, or an event—and scoped the room. If there was a cute guy, the first thing we did was check to see if he had a ring on his left hand. If he didn't, that still didn't prove he was single, but we assumed he was. From there, we let happen what will happen—a little eye contact, a smile, flirting, maybe a conversation and a possible date. And we still do it that way from time to time.

But now, with the Internet, chat rooms, and online dating services, there are all kinds of opportunities to get connected. And you don't even have to get dressed up. You could be in your bathrobe looking like death warmed over while getting acquainted with someone online. Based on your words and the picture you posted, he could think you're the hottest thing since sliced bread. If he could only see you now. Honestly, if you were to get on various dating sites, it could become a full-time job just responding to e-mails, reading profiles, and weeding through all the possibilities.

Although Michelle has found her dream man (and she didn't meet him online), I (Connie) have been going solo. Honestly, I don't know what's harder at this stage of life, finding a health insurance policy or connecting with the right man, especially when both of us, after living half a century and beyond, have more baggage than a 747.

Dating after marriage is not what any of us expected. Some of us have been living the married life for quite some time, and suddenly we find ourselves in need of a tune-up. Many of us rush to the gym to lose weight, to the mall to embrace the latest fashion trends, to the salon to cover the gray and hit up some highlights, and to learn how to discuss something other than our children and how our marriages fell apart.

Instead of dating, we should be taking time to heal, but that's not typically what women do after divorce. Each of us has to go through our own journey, which might take us down the same painful path over and over again until we get it right.

Michelle and I (Connie) have had our share of good and bad online dating experiences, and we want to share what we've learned along the way.

ADVENTURES OF ONLINE DATING

Connie

It has been ten years since my twenty-six-year marriage shockingly ended. I didn't see it coming. And after two serious relationships with men that left me completely shattered and a host of other short-term relationships, I had a meeting with my accountant, who is also a good friend. She asked how my love life was going, and after I gave her my latest sob story, she said in her bubbly, Southern voice, "Sweetie, you need to go on Match.com." That's where she met her husband. Before I knew it, she had her camera out. She started shooting photos of me and had me signed up before I left the office. All I had to do was go home and fill out the profile questions. So, without any intention of doing so, I ended up on an online dating service, which I affectionately refer to as Match.CON. (No, I don't mean Con as in con-artist. It's a play on words because my name is Connie.)

I did it for six months. After going through pictures and pro-files, I decided I would make the monetary investment worth my while by meeting all the men I thought I had common ground with on what I considered important issues.

There are some things you must do before the big meet up.

The first thing is to establish your headquarters. In other words, where are you going to meet these guys? You should choose a public place, just to be safe. My headquarters was every Starbucks within a twenty-mile radius of my home.

The second thing you must do is come up with your out. This means that if after one coffee and thirty minutes of chatting, you decide this isn't going to work out, you need a way of vamoosing. So come up with a believable excuse, such as, "I'd really like to stay longer, but I have to get home and walk the dog (wash my hair, pour hot tar up my nostrils)." You get the idea.

The third thing you must do is figure out what your deal-breakers are. Here are a couple of examples of mine: If he's separated but not divorced, fuhgeddaboudit. If he's an addict or he's living at home with his mother until he reestablishes him-self, no way José.

Figure out *why* you are getting on a dating site. Not everyone gets on for the same reason you do. Some people want to make friends. Some want to make business contacts. Some want a dating relationship that will never go further than that. Some want companionship. Some are looking for a romp in the hay or friends with benefits. And then there are those who are actually looking for a potential lifelong mate they are willing to tie the knot with. That was me. I was looking for the latter. I wanted that special someone I would connect with spiritually, intellectually, emotionally, and on the same playing field financially who was marriage potential. And, oh yes, someone who was physically appealing to me. Anyone who tries to tell you that physical attraction is not important is not being honest. It is, indeed. It's not the most important thing in a relationship, but it is necessary.

I couldn't believe some of the pictures that were posted on Match.com. I'm of Italian heritage, born and raised in Chicago, and living in the mid-south. The differences in culture showed up in the photos. I'd liken it to *My Cousin Vinny's* Mona Lisa Vito (not quite) looking for her match in Alabama. You wouldn't think five hundred miles (the distance between Chicago and Nashville) could make that big of a difference culturally, but it does. As Aunt Voula says in *My Big Fat Greek Wedding*, "That why that no work."

Another thing that baffled me about the pictures is the men who would post pictures of sunsets, airplanes, forests, and various other things. Why? Is this to show us their photography skills? And some of them would be in pictures with several different attractive women. Are you kidding me? Why in the world would you post pictures of yourself on a dating service with a bunch of beautiful women? I still haven't figured that one out—unless they were looking for someone else to join the party, if you know what I mean. Since we are talking about pictures, post *recent* pictures of yourself. Don't post pictures taken five-plus years ago. Believe me, you've changed.

Actually, I felt uncomfortable with the whole online dating thing of telling about myself and posting my picture. I felt like I was selling myself on eBay or Craigslist. And in the searching process, I felt like I was shopping for a guy like I would shop for a car. But that's how dating is done in the twenty-first century. My grandparents were set up with each other; that's how it was done years ago. And for some reason, most of those marriages seemed to work. But my grandchildren may be looking for their potential mates online. The world is changing rapidly.

There's a section in your profile where you can list your favorite book. So I said, "*Live, Love, Laugh Again.* I should know: I'm one of the authors." Do you know that out of all the men who contacted me, only three caught that bit of information, researched it, and realized that I really was one of the authors? Men are highly visual, so I don't think the profile information is what matters most to them.

I must tell you that the Delete button is very important in your search. A girl can be bombarded with e-mails. Once you look at the profile and photos of the person making contact, you can decide whether or not to communicate with him. If I decided that I didn't want further communication, I would send him an e-mail thanking him for taking the time to write and state my reason for the deletion like, "Motorcycles aren't my thing." And then I'd hit Delete. If a guy couldn't form a sentence, spelled like a third grader, or had way too many grammatical errors in his writing, he'd automatically get deleted. It's just a quirk I have.

I was looking for someone within a range of five years younger or five years older than I. I stated that I was not interested in having any more children. Yet I would get e-mails from men who were the same age as my older daughter. Their profiles would clearly state they were seeking women her age and wanted children. And of course, most of them were eye candy. I'd chuckle and write these guys a brief note and say something like, "I'm really flattered that you took the time to write, but did you check out my profile? I'm probably your mother's age." Then I'd delete them.

Now let's go on a few adventures with some of the men I met online. I have changed their names and geographical details to protect them.

Brad the Blast

I showed up at my headquarters where I was to meet Brad, an attorney. He described himself as athletic and toned. Yet I wondered why every picture he posted was only from the neck up. He was already there when I arrived, and he had on gym shorts, a T-shirt, gym shoes, and a whistle around his neck. I thought, *Couldn't he throw on a pair of jeans and a decent shirt and lose the whistle?* He said he'd just gotten done working out. Athletic and toned, huh? He did have huge biceps and shoulders, but let's just say it was obvious that Brad pumped a lot of iron but didn't do much cardio.

We ordered our coffees and began to talk. But *he* did all the talking. As a matter of fact, he didn't come up for air. He said, "Ya know, I have two sons, and we play basketball together and goof around a lot. We have a Blast. Just a Blast." The way he said "blast" was with an amplified *B*. "Yeah, I love the guys I work with, we just have a Blast at the office. A bunch of us go to the nursing home once a month, and we meet with some of the old folks. We just have a Blast! I just bought a brand-new house and I've been having a Blast decorating the place. Just like a little kid in a candy store. A Blast! I love my church. I'm in a great Sunday school class. We have so much fun. It's a Blast!"

He didn't ask me one question about myself. (Hint: If he doesn't ask anything about you, he's probably too self-centered.) Well, he just went on blasting himself into oblivion while I was thinking, *What am I doing here? I'd rather be having a root canal right now.*

I went home and imagined what life would be like with Brad the Blast. I pictured myself in the kitchen and imagined him walking in the door. He says, "Hi, honey, how was your day?" And I say, "Not the best, I had a flat tire this afternoon and had a bit of a headache." And he says, "No worries, baby, let's get cozy. We'll have a Blast!" With that I pictured him taking off his shirt, and I saw that whistle around his neck. Then I hit Delete!

Sal the Teacher

When I arrived at my headquarters, Sal was already there sporting his Bermuda shorts with socks and sandals. A fashion plate, he wasn't. He looked exactly like his picture, which was a good thing. We made small talk, ordered our coffees, and sat down.

I asked him questions to get the conversation going. "What's life like as a teacher?" He said, "I teach all day, work with students individually who need extra help, grade papers, go to in-service meetings, and what-have-you." I asked him what he did for fun. "Well, I like to go to movies, go for walks, work in the yard, read a book, and what-have-you." I asked him what kind of food he liked. "I'm not a picky eater. I eat oatmeal for breakfast, go out for a burger once a week, and just eat what's in the fridge, and what-have-you." This guy's favorite ending for almost every sentence was "what-have-you." It drove me completely bonkers. He didn't laugh. He was a serious guy.

So I went home and pictured myself in the kitchen. He comes home from work and I say, "Hi, honey, what did you do today?" He blandly says, "I had my oatmeal, went to school, taught the kids, had lunch, graded papers, just the usual, and what-have-you." I then picture myself with my hands around his neck, saying, "If you say 'what-have-you' one more time, that's it!" So to keep from hurting anyone, I hit Delete!

Paul from Mayberry

I was very excited about meeting Paul. He was handsome and seemed to be a successful businessman. We lived in close proximity to each other. We communicated via e-mail, and he seemed to write intelligently. The big mistake was not talking to him before we met. It's probably because I do voice-over work that I have a habit of listening to voices, and I'm attracted to that in a man. If he has a nice voice, it's a big plus.

When I walked into my headquarters, I saw him sitting there. He was every bit as handsome in person as he was in his picture. He immediately recognized me and stood up from his chair and said loudly, "You must be Connie! Would you like a cappuccino, a latte, or a mocha?" He talked like Gomer Pyle from the *Andy Griffith Show*. Now, please, don't get me wrong. I love a nice Southern drawl, but I'm not attracted to the accent of guys from Mayberry.

I immediately cringed at the sound of his voice. I sat across from him and wanted to say, "Be quiet and let me look at you." He was pleasing to the eye, but it ended right there. We talked about restaurants as he talked loudly in his Gomer-esque voice. "I love sports bars. Do you like sports bars, Connie? I generally like to sit at the bar, not at the tables." It went downhill from there. I really tried to let the whole voice thing go because there were other things I liked about him.

But I went home and pictured myself in the kitchen. He walks in the door, and I think, *My husband is so handsome.* But then the loud, Gomer Pyle–voice takes over and ruins everything. I wince at the sound of it. I have to hit Delete!

Nino the Italian

After the Midwestern-girl-meets-Mayberry-guy glitch, I decided it was time to try to connect with someone who was more like me, someone from my neck of the woods. And if he was Italian, we'd surely have a lot in common just talking about our families. So Nino contacted me. He was a good-looking guy from Pennsylvania. He was a musician, so we had that in common. Talking music is always great fun.

Nino and I had great phone conversations. We talked about how we make our spaghetti sauces and other things Italian. And a big plus—I liked his voice very much. So I was excited about meeting him. When we met at my headquarters, he looked nice and a lot like his picture. We had a good time bantering back and forth, but I soon realized that things wouldn't work for us because he was between jobs and didn't know what he was going to do next. He was in a huge financial bind because of his divorce. He really wanted to be a successful songwriter. I know the likelihood of hitting it big in the music industry is slim, and at my age I didn't want to wait around while he was trying to figure it out. (If I were twenty, it might have been a different story.)

When it was time to leave, he walked me to my car and tried to kiss me. I was taken aback because none of the other guys had been as bold as Nino. I put my hand up to block the kiss and said, "No, I'm not ready for that now." He looked at me with his hands up in the air and said, "Wha . . . you're not going to kiss me?" He sounded somewhat like Robert De Niro in a Mafia flick. I couldn't believe it. I said, "I've known you for one hour, and you want to lock lips?" He was disgusted and looked at me as if to say, *What's wrong with you?* I have no question in my mind that he deleted me before I could get home and picture myself in the kitchen.

Adam the Alias

Of all the guys I came in contact with, Adam was probably the most attractive guy. Our first meeting was so successful that I decided I would go on a second date with him, and I was hopeful. Our first dinner date was good, so when he called at the spur of the moment one day when I was shopping with my daughter and invited me to dinner, my daughter joined us. She thought he was okay. On the third date, things felt a little off. I'd really been happy thus far and thought maybe there could be something there.

Then he said, "I need to talk to you about something." Immediately, my heart sank. I've heard those words before and what followed wasn't pretty at all. He proceeded to tell me that he wasn't who he said he was. His real name was John Doe, but he had changed his identity because someone had ripped off a million dollars from him. He had given himself a new name and made it so he was unable to be found. No one could find out any personal information about him if they tried.

This was a little too much for me to handle, and I told him so.

Then I went home and pictured myself in the kitchen. Every time he comes in the house, I wonder when he's going to drop the next big bomb on me, like, "Oh, honey, I forgot to tell you, I have a wife and two kids on the East Coast." I just have to hit Delete!

Cal the Cutie

Cal was really handsome. He took great care of himself, and I really admire that in a man. So I was happy when I entered my headquarters and saw him for the first time. We had a lovely conversation, and I thought I'd really like to see him again to find out more about him. He seemed to have a great relationship with God and knew a lot about the Bible. If a guy plays that card with me, I'm usually drawn to him.

Then we talked a little bit about our past marriages. I don't like to hang on that subject for a long time, but it's good to talk about it some. He proceeded to tell me about the nightmare he was living in. He told me that his wife had him arrested from his place of employment, much to his shock, and accused him of spousal abuse. Their case was going to the grand jury.

My head was spinning. I couldn't believe it. Needless to say, there was no going home and picturing myself in the kitchen.

Phil the Control Freak

Phil was a Southern gentleman who was extremely successful as a property investor. He'd been married for close to thirty years and divorced for three years. I deviated off my Starbucks track and met him at Dunkin' Donuts. I had less than an hour to spare as I had a business appointment, and Phil was disappointed that I couldn't stay longer. Our initial meeting went well, so I agreed to have dinner with him the following week.

He called me later that day and gave me an assignment. He asked me if I had read *The Five Love Languages*. I hadn't. So he said, "Here's what I want you to do. I want you to go to Barnes & Noble and pick up a copy of *The Five Love Languages*. Then go into the coffee shop and get a coffee and read the last few pages. Decide which two love languages describe you best and let me know." I was turned off by the instructions he gave me. It was as if he were talking to one of his kids or an employee or someone he could give orders to. But I thought I'd not be too quick to judge and decided to meet him for dinner anyway. (Another note: never let him come to pick you up on the first date. Be cautious and play it safe. Always drive separately. You don't know who this guy is yet.)

The dinner was fine, but I noticed that he talked to me in the third person the entire evening, saying things like, "Phil is physically attracted to Connie. Connie looks beautiful tonight. Phil likes it when . . ." I thought that was really odd and annoying.

We went out for coffee after dinner and sat outside. It was a beautiful summer evening, and I was leaning in toward the table, engaged in our conversation, when he said, "Phil would like to see Connie more often if Connie could fit him into her schedule." You see, he'd been trying to see me during the week, and I was too busy to make it. I'm usually not a spur-of-the-moment gal. Most of the time I book things in advance. When he said that, I pulled back from the table, and he said, "Phil does not like Connie's body language."

I said, "Connie does not like being told what to do. This isn't going to work out for her." With that, I thanked him for the great dinner and spending time with me—but that was it. Deletion happened before the kitchen routine.

George from St. Louis

I was visiting my friend in St. Louis, and it just happened that I had been communicating with a man from there. Since I was in the area, we decided to meet for a coffee. After all my unsuccessful attempts at connecting with divorced men, I decided I'd really like to meet George because he was a widower. We had a lovely conversation, and he was very attractive. He was successful in his work, and he'd traveled the world.

The conversation was engaging, and since he'd come quite a ways to see me, I spent more time with him than usual. So we got around to talking about his wife, his marriage, and how she had passed. Are you ready for this one? He told me she had drowned in the bathtub. I know this must have been horrifying for him. But all I thought was, *Connie, you don't know this guy, and this is just way too weird. He could be telling the truth about how it happened... but maybe not.*

Sheesh! How many more weird situations could I run into? A guy who changes his identity, a guy whose case is going to the grand jury for spousal abuse, and now the widower whose wife drowned in the bathtub. This completely freaked me out.

So I went home and pictured myself in the kitchen. He comes home from work and asks me how my day was. I say, "I'm a little sore from my workout today." He says, "No problem, honey, I'll run a nice warm bath for you." I couldn't hit Delete fast enough.

• • •

There were two other gentlemen I met whom I would've been interested in a second date with based on the great conversations we had and physical attraction, but they deleted me when they realized they weren't going to hit a home run that night.

During that time I also met four other gentlemen I thought were great guys. We connected on a lot of important issues. The only problem was that I didn't feel there was any chemistry. After the cake is baked and all the right ingredients are in it, it's the frosting that makes it really special. And that's how it is with chemistry. The guys had qualities I admired, but the chemistry wasn't there so there was no reason to take it any further. Pity.

Now let me tell you about a few friends who also had some online dating experiences they shared with me and didn't mind me passing their stories along to you.

Lee is a physical therapist. He's a great guy, more on the serious side, but you can get him to let his hair down once in a while. He connected with a woman on Couples.com and then met her for coffee. Thank goodness it wasn't dinner. When his date showed up, he noticed that she didn't have any teeth. Are you kidding me? You can show up without mascara. But you can't show up without teeth. She shared with him that she'd had some surgery and was waiting for a plate to be made. I don't care if she would've looked like Angelina Jolie without a full set of teeth, did she really think Lee would want to go out with her again? Yikes!

Then there's Manny. Manny is more of a serious guy too and kind of shy but a real sweetheart. It takes a lot to get him to put himself out there. But he decided to go online to see if he could connect with that special someone. He was amazed by the number of women who made the initial contact, and several of them didn't make any bones about wanting a sexual relationship. They told him that he needed to come to the date prepared with sufficient protection . . . just in case. Seriously?

After having a few conversations with a lady, Manny decided it was time to meet face-to-face. Manny noticed that she looked kind of sick. As they discussed various topics, she shared with him that she'd been diagnosed with Lyme disease. But she was relieved that it was only Lyme disease because at first the doctors thought she was mentally ill. It kind of went downhill from there. Manny decided not to pursue that one.

Then there's my friend Gail. Gail's husband passed away, and she decided to go online to see if she could meet a widower. She met a man from Arizona, about two thousand miles away from where she lived. I don't know his name, so we'll just call him Mike. She and Mike talked every night for almost one year before meeting. She saw his photos on Match.com and received e-mails and phone calls daily. She loved everything about him. He pushed all the right buttons and said all the right things. They really hit it off. However, she'd never met him in person.

After six months or so, they were saying, "I love you" to each other. She knew she was in love with the man on the other end of the phone. Almost one year later, they were talking marriage so she decided to take a trip to Phoenix. She planned to resign from her job and put her house on the market to move there. She bought some new clothes, got herself all dolled up, the whole nine yards. She wanted to look her best when she met Mike. When she arrived in Phoenix, he was to pick her up at the airport. She looked all over for him and couldn't find him. Finally, he came up to her . . . looking nothing like his picture. He was much older and much heavier. After having lunch with him, she told him he'd lied to her by not posting current photos. She took the next plane back home. End of story. Almost a whole year wasted.

Then there's my friend Shawn. She thought she hit the jackpot with Ryan. The first several dates went extremely well, and she brought him home to meet her parents. He seemed quite normal for a while. Then he began stalking Shawn everywhere she went. He hacked into her Facebook account and other personal accounts. He would make sick posts on her Facebook page, and I knew Shawn would never post anything like that. He was able somehow to get some of her money. He was able to control everything in her personal life. He made threats. She had to get the police involved and put a restraining order on him. It was an ugly mess. Shawn was terrified, and it affected her so badly, she thought about moving out of town and starting a new life somewhere else. A background check is nice if you're really starting to get serious. It's a shame we have to resort to this today, but at least we have the means to do it for a little added protection.

This by far is the online dating story that takes the cake! A guy decided to meet a woman he'd been communicating with. She was every bit as lovely as her photos. As they began to talk, he noticed that she kept putting her hand in her purse and putting something in her mouth. The something was toilet paper. She confessed that she was addicted to it and consumed around a roll a day. Needless to say, but I'll say it anyway, there was no second date. He really should've thought about it, though. She probably owns stock in White Cloud, Angel Soft, and Charmin.

But not all stories are horror stories.

There's my friend Wanda. Wanda is extremely attractive. She's a professional woman with a lot of class. She's very confident and charming. She decided to get on Match.com, narrowed down her eighty pursuers to twelve, and decided to meet them all in one weekend. Wanda doesn't mess around. She had one coffee date after the next. Honestly, I don't know how she drank that many coffees in two days. But it was worth it all because the last one she met had a definite connection with her. The chemistry was there. They've been dating seriously for several years, and now they are engaged. There are success stories with online dating. I guess if it's in God's plan for your life, you will find the right match.

That's the key right there. Are you willing to stay the course and weed through guy after guy, making sure not to back down from what's really important to you in a relationship? The decision is yours.

Before Michelle gives her take on this topic, I have to share with you one of the funniest cards I ever received from a dear friend after one of my wrenching heartbreaks. The front of the card says, "Waiting for the Perfect Man." Then there's a picture of a lovely park with a bench. Sitting on the bench is a woman dressed to the nines, sporting a red dress, great shoes, leopard shawl, every hair in place, jewelry, and she's with her small dog. But both she and the dog are corpses. I laughed till I cried.

WILL THE REAL YOU PLEASE STAND UP?

Michelle

Connie definitely cornered the market there for a while when it comes to online dating. My experience doesn't come close to hers. However, I have a few thoughts and stories to share that may help you in your journey.

Online connecting can be enticing because it seems low risk.

While we are suddenly now members of the lonely hearts' club, let's be careful not to let our wisdom fly out the window just to hear a voice on the other end of the line.

I came out of my divorce with virtually no friends, and especially no single friends. All my friends were married, and I didn't even have any girlfriends. As I shared earlier, I knew no one at the time who had gone through a divorce, so the initial loneliness was unbearable.

Like Connie, a friend of mine who had met her spouse on Match.com encouraged me to get online and start dating. Like most of you, I found it strange to be putting my profile, which included intimate details of my life, out there for the whole world to see. It seemed wrong for some reason, yet many of my friends had found great success in it.

At first, the onslaught of e-mails from men was flattering, but then I realized how much time it took to return them and to sift through the ones who were not even close to a match. The whole thing became way too much for me to approach from a dating perspective. So I changed my mission to a friend-finding mission, and it immediately eliminated a lot of guys. I actually ended up meeting some great guy friends on Match.com who remain good friends today. It was definitely an unexpected surprise. The online dating services really weren't my thing.

You don't have to use an online dating service these days to meet a guy online. I met someone through Facebook. His profile looked great. We seemed to have a lot in common. We started with the chat feature. He asked me some random question, and I responded. I could tell just by our conversation that he was someone I wanted to know more about. At some point we moved from chat to phone and began talking.

Our conversations were long . . . two to three hours sometimes. We'd talk about everything, and he was filling me up emotionally and spiritually. Some of our time on the phone was prayer time. I think the prayer time is what really got me. I had never prayed so much with a man, and it was so impressive. What I didn't realize is I was becoming very intimate with him through the times we would pray together.

In every other area I was taking it slow, not opening my heart too much, but when we prayed my heart was totally open and vulnerable. Just a quick word of warning: until you know you are going to marry someone, having long prayer times with a man should not be on your get-to-know-you list. Prayer is deeply connecting your heart to another and is an intimate act of worship. It should be reserved for when you know you are going to spend the rest of your life with someone, because it can easily open other doors of intimacy on a physical level without you even realizing it.

After a couple of months of talking on the phone, we arranged to meet. By this time my heart was so open to this man I was sure he was someone I'd end up in a serious relationship with once we were able to know one another in person.

Well, a disappointing thing happened. We met, we embraced, and I did not connect. It was so crazy. I had talked to him for two months and felt so close to this man, yet when I met him in person I was not remotely attracted to him. But he had planned a romantic date for us, so I wasn't going to leave. The next evening I thought maybe I'd feel differently, but nothing. In fact, over dinner he began to say some very strange things that made me realize I had made a big mistake. Red flags were everywhere, but even then, I didn't quite bail out yet.

Needless to say, the two and a half months were an illusion. This man was totally different from what he appeared to be on the phone. My suggestion is if your dating relationship starts out on the phone, keep it friends. Don't have any expectations or give him any until after you meet. It could have turned out great, but even then, we were too far ahead of ourselves before we even met. Also, make sure to take it slow once you do meet. Women, you know we are easily drawn in emotionally with words. Words mean nothing unless they are backed with action. You need to see this man live out everything you talked about before you let your heart start opening up.

My online experience was brief, two months to be exact, but in the short time I was online I met some great friends—and one of those friends introduced me to a man I ended up dating for a fairly long time. I do believe in the midst of the mix there are some gems. Here are some of my suggestions to help you eliminate, or as Con says, delete.

1. Set your standards high and do not deviate.
2. Start off with e-mail, move to phone, and then move to a date. Make sure to ask the right questions so you don't waste your time meeting him in person. I encourage you to have your questions written down.
3. The hardest thing for divorced women is to realize there are no perfect men. While your standards are high, if his personality plays well or his character stands out, be willing to compromise some.
4. Always, always, always meet in a public place. Never have him pick you up from your home. You never know who is on the other end of the phone or e-mail.

5. Don't be afraid to ask for references.

6. Don't meet for dinner right away. Start with coffee or tea.

7. Always ask for a photo. My first Match.com connection did not have a photo. I spent hours e-mailing him and finally met him for coffee only to realize I was not remotely attracted to him. I felt terrible having to backtrack the relationship as a result.

8. Stick to men who live close to home so you can confirm his integrity through others. If he's in some other city, he may have a whole separate life he isn't telling you about (I've seen this happen more than once), and you will never know until after you are too far down the road.

Facebook is a whole different world than Match.com. Your defenses are down because somehow you were connected through a friend. The problem is, most of us don't know which friend or even how closely they know each other. Make sure to do your due diligence here too. It's easy to become enamored with the postings of someone and his interaction on Facebook, only to find out he is not the person he is portraying.

It only happened once to me, but I did fall head over heels for a Facebook friend, and it was a lesson learned. I did some due diligence checking him out with other friends but didn't guard my heart the way I should have. We connected via phone on an emotional level so deeply that by the time we met in person I was totally crazy about him and did not see some of the warning signs. It was a quick run, but I could have been in real trouble if I had been in a more vulnerable place.

Make sure no matter who knows him, and no matter how many friends you have in common, you still use the same set of standards and safety measures as you would on online dating sites.

In the short time I dated online, I had a few phone conversations that eliminated things quickly. One gentleman became very angry with me when I had something come up with the kids and could not talk very long. Actually, he was more than angry; he was irate. Obviously we never had another conversation.

The other thing I noticed is that the men online are most likely pursuing your other available, local friends too. There are only so many guys in one city, and if they are online, and you and your girlfriends are online, make sure to beware. They could have a date the very next night with one of your friends.

Also, take note of how long they have been on the dating website. There are some who are serial social media daters. They never get off because their only goal is to find someone vulnerable enough to take to dinner and get into bed with. Divorced women, and particularly women who have suffered abuse or neglect, are the perfect targets for predators. Be careful, and take notice of these things as you enter this new world of dating.

Most of the men I met online were not really who they said they were. I am notorious for asking lots of questions (my journalistic background), and I would find that while they would list one thing about themselves online, in person it became clear that thing was not true. I also realized the word *Christian* is thrown around very loosely. Before you meet in person, I'd ask him to define what his beliefs are and what Christianity means to him. You don't want to waste time meeting with someone who holds different values.

Overall, my summary would be that though I didn't find the love of my life online, I did find some good friends who are still friends today. So don't throw out the whole idea; just be extra careful as you proceed.

YOU and Dating Thoughts

Online dating did not work for us, and the conclusion we came to is while we met some good friends, it wasn't our place for meeting Mr. Right. However, we have friends who have used online dating services and social media to meet men and have wonderful stories to tell, so don't rule it out completely. After our episodes of experience in the online world, we do think you should proceed with serious caution.

YOU and Dating Actions

- Set your sights high.
- What are your deal-breakers? Define them.
- It's easy to talk on the phone, e-mail back and forth, and become emotionally connected only to find when you meet in person there is no physical attraction, or the person you thought you knew is not the person you actually meet. So guard your heart. Do not pursue a relationship just because he sounds good and says all the things you want to hear on the phone. Be a little skeptical, and see if he makes the effort to meet you in person. If he's cool with the phone thing for a long time, then he's not the type of guy who will commit.
- If he talks only about himself, says nothing about his

kids or his family, is on the outs with his parents, or
hasn't spoken to his siblings in years, cut the cord.

- Find out his side of the story as to why his marriage
failed. If the guy blames his ex-wife for everything,
calls her names, or puts her down, then the answer is a
resounding no. If he is this angry, if he has not seen his
own sin in the situation and has absolutely no remorse
or sadness for the demise of the marriage or owned
his responsibility in the breakup, then he's not ready to
move on.
- If he doesn't have a job and is up to his eyeballs in
debt, don't consider him. Why would you want to add
more stress to your life?
- If the guy is pushy in any way and trying to take
things faster than you are comfortable with, then he's
probably desperate and not ready to be in a healthy
relationship.
- Never, ever let a guy pick you up at your house on the
first date. Meet him somewhere in a relatively busy
area of town, not too far from where you live.
- If you really like the guy and want to take the
relationship to the next level, do a background check.
As women, we want to believe in a fairy-tale romance.
We want to trust with our whole hearts and souls.
But there are predators out there who can smell the
next victim a mile away. This doesn't mean that you're
looking for a perfect man. But you're not looking for an
ex-convict, addict, or a Jekyll and Hyde. A lot can be
said of a background check, and at least you can have
peace of mind knowing he is not a criminal.

- Follow your gut instinct. And remember, if it smells fishy, it is. If it seems like things don't add up, they don't. When in doubt—*don't*!
- Once you do meet someone you want to invest some time into, introduce him to every friend you have and get their feedback. It's easy to see him through rose-colored glasses when you're in the gaga stage. You need those outside eyes to see who's really there. And don't forget to take it slow.
- Look for history. History with friends, history with family, and even church references would be good. See how he reacts to others and how they react to him.

YOU and Dating Prayer

Lord, give me wisdom as I enter this new world of online dating. Your protection, Your guidance is so important as I walk this path. Lord, You know the hearts of men. You know all things. I know only what I see. Reveal the hearts of men to me, and help me discern those who are not who they say they are. Help me be patient and, if I am to marry again, if this is part of Your plan for my life, use Your wisdom in walking out relationships in a discerning and godly way. Thank You, Lord, for watching over me. In Jesus' name, amen.

five

YOU AND SEX

We hate to, but we feel like we need to address the subject of sexual relationships outside of marriage. It's such a personal and private thing. But this book is about real issues we deal with as divorced, single, Christian women. In doing so, we're going to be very candid about our own lives and what we've learned about this topic after divorce. Not having sex is a tough thing to grasp after divorce. After all, you've been used to having sex in your marriage, and now that you're divorced, you're supposed to turn off the "I want sex" button. But if you're a believer, then you know that the Bible says sex outside of marriage is not God's will. And we're not going to go over all the verses with you about sexual immorality, lust, fornication, and adultery. It's all right there in black and white and sometimes red. We didn't write it; it's God's Word.

However, many of us rewrite the Bible to fit our lifestyles. We bargain with God and think, *If I do nine really great things out of ten, then I can get away with this one little sin.* We think, *God is merciful. If I repent, He'll forgive me.* And according to the Bible,

He will. But why does God tell us not to have sexual relationships outside of marriage? All too often, we find that Christian women rush into marriage relationships without going through the healing process simply because they don't want to have sex outside of marriage. They don't want to have that sin hanging over their heads. But what's worse? Getting married right away so you can have sex without feeling guilty, or going through another divorce because you rushed into another marriage?

This subject is a bit complicated because God did create us to be sexual beings. We desire relationship with each other, and when things get serious between two people, physical intimacy is wanted and needed. It's a natural progression. And God loves the sexual relationship between a man and a woman . . . in the right circumstances. We know sexuality is a tough subject, and that is why we knew we couldn't leave out this chapter. It's probably one of the toughest things women have to deal with in life after divorce, and, like everything else we've shared, we want to help you navigate through this issue.

LOOKING FOR A MAND-AID

Connie

I've always been one to tell it like it is, and I'm not going to stop now. We thought about naming this chapter "Sexless in the Suburbs" as it relates or un-relates to the show *Sex and the City*. I admit I watched this show. Not that I condone the sexual lifestyle and promiscuity of the four single women the show portrays, but I loved the fashion; the whole feel of living in New York City as a single, professional woman, and the relationship between the four girlfriends. They knew everything about one another and were there for each other. They lent an ear, gave advice, and were each other's confidants. I love that. It almost brings me back to the idea of the Con-Vent. Even though it's very different, something about it is oddly the same.

If I haven't shocked you yet, I'll shock you now. If I were God, I'd probably say, "If you're divorced, you don't have to ever get married again. In fact, you probably shouldn't. Just date whoever's a good fit for you. Be in a serious relationship with one person if you want to. Have sex with him if you want to. You're a big girl. You know what you're doing. Don't try to mesh families, money, kids, and emotional baggage after divorce. You've been there, done that. Just stay single, and do your own thing your way." Can you believe I just said that? It's a good thing I'm not God! But that's how many of us decide to do life after divorce. And some of us are very happy doing it that way. I will share my own story and why that didn't work for me.

I want to tell you about a serious relationship I got into after the ink barely dried on my divorce decree. After being married for twenty-six years and going through an unwanted divorce, I was completely vulnerable and made decisions based purely on my emotions. I wasn't engaging my brain in the decision process, especially regarding men. I was way too wounded. So when a woman is wounded, what does she need? My friend Val calls it a mand-aid. Brilliant, Val! Not a Band-Aid, but a mand-aid to stop the bleeding.

All the experts tell you to let the dust settle. Wait before doing anything big. Don't move right away. Don't make big purchases. Don't get into a dating relationship with anyone. The first thing to do after any major life change is to figure out where you are, take a deep breath, and take the time to heal. For crying out loud, going through my divorce was like getting broadsided by a train going two hundred miles per hour. I was completely shattered. You can't put yourself back together again in a few months. But that's exactly what I tried to do. Since healing takes awhile, most of us get impatient and don't want to take the time needed to do it. How I wish I had. It's all right, though. God's in the beauty-for-ashes business (Isaiah 61:3). And He uses every rotten thing we get ourselves into for our good. It's amazing how He does that. It took me walking this road to get to where I am today, which is a much better place.

Earlier I mentioned Brandon. I had known him for quite some time. He contacted me because he heard through the grapevine that my husband had left me, and he wanted me to know that he had gone through the same thing. So we began to console each other. We'd cry on each other's shoulders about the demise of our marriages.

Our e-mails led to phone calls. Phone calls led to visits. Visits led to him doing "guy things" around the house that needed tending to or one of us using any lame excuse to get together. Visits led to dates, and before long we were joined at the hip only three months after my divorce was finalized. And I fell hopelessly, or should I say hopefully, in love with him. Let me add this little bit of info. Brandon was considerably younger than I. Can we say "eye candy"? At least in my eyes he was. I know this sounds so superficial. But I wasn't thinking clearly at all. Please realize that my brain went on vacation during this time, and I was back in teenage mode. All the feelings I thought had gone away forever had resurfaced, and I didn't know what to do with them. For all those years I'd been with my husband, who was close to my own age, and now this young guy who was attracted to me came into my life. I mean, what's a wounded girl supposed to do, right? Dive right in and, in the process, almost drown. That's what!

I'm not going to go into all the details, but one thing led to another. We had a long relationship filled with intimacy. We were there for each other . . . always. Because we were so crazy about each other, we crossed the line (according to God's Word) sexually. But we did not have intercourse. This was the way we tried to get around it, by not going the full distance. We think we can do all the precursors to the deed, but if we don't do the actual deed, then we're safe. That was me. Bill Clinton's famous line will always be remembered: "I did not have sex with that woman." But you can be having sex with someone without going the distance.

Let me give you a different analogy. You filled the bathtub with water. You stood right next to the tub with your clothes off, and you put your sponge and soap in the water and washed yourself completely, but you didn't get in the tub. Did you take a bath or not? Not really, but your mission was accomplished. I close my case. It was stupid. Stupid on one side because I wasn't kidding God. I was trying to kid myself. Stupid on the other side because being sexually intimate with Brandon caused me to have a soul tie that I couldn't shake loose. It took me a long time to get over him after our breakup because of the sexual intimacy I'd had with him. Ah . . . an epiphany . . . I get it now! That's why God says it's not a good idea to have a sexual relationship with a man who is not your husband. It will hurt you so badly in the end when it doesn't work out, and it'll take you much longer to get past the heartbreak because your souls are connected. One of the best books I ever read on this subject was one that I actually narrated, so buy the audio book if you can. It's called *Sex and the Soul of a Woman* by Paula Rinehart.[1] This is a book filled with truths. I saw myself in so many places, and it really gave me clarity.

It's important for me to say that even though I was happy in my relationship with Brandon, I was miserable in my relationship with God. I had a strong conviction about what I was doing. I felt like I was leading a double life: faithful to Brandon but unfaithful to the Lover of my soul. Faithful to the one who left me in the end, but unfaithful to the One who tells me He'll never leave me or forsake me. I was miserable in church every week because I knew what I'd done the night before. I believe it was the conviction of the Holy Spirit. I couldn't keep living like that. That's why after almost four years of dating, I pushed the issue of getting married. "Please make me an honest woman," I said. He agreed to it, but in the end, he couldn't go through with it. You see, Brandon hadn't taken the time he needed for healing after his divorce either, and even though he loved me, he didn't love me enough to tie the knot again. And thank God he didn't. Because after all the newlywed stuff had worn off, we probably would've realized that we weren't the best match—which is why 65 percent of second marriages end in divorce.

I went through such pain and anguish over that breakup. Why? Because I didn't take the time I needed to heal from my marriage ending and because I had a soul tie with another man that kept me bound for many years. It took much prayer, counseling, and lots of time to get over him. I repented before God. I repented to Brandon for being halfway responsible for taking us both to a place we shouldn't have gone. I repented to my adult daughters for setting a poor example in living a lifestyle I knew wasn't pleasing to God. I wasn't pulling the wool over their eyes. I was so disappointed in myself. I know. It sounds as though I was filled with guilt and beat myself up. I did for a while. But then I realized how much God loves me. I've moved on. I've forgiven myself, and God has forgiven me. I'm happy to report I'm in a good place now.

Financial expert Dave Ramsey says he gives you the same advice your grandmother would, except he keeps his teeth in. Well, my sweet grandma from Italy gave me some great advice that I didn't listen to. When I started dating as a young girl, she sat me down and told me in her broken English, "Listen here, Concetina (my name in Italian), you're not supposed to do da job (have sex) with a man if he's not your husband. He no respect you if you do da job with him." Then when I was about to get married, she sat me down again, and this time she said, "If your husband wants to do da job, you gotta do it whenever he wants to. Because that's your job! Don't you say you're too tired or you have a head-ache. He's supposed to give you a piece of bread (support you financially), and you're supposed to always be ready, willing, and able to do da job on demand." Ah, if life were that easy. He brings home the bread and butter, and you fulfill his need. Sounds old-fashioned, doesn't it? But there is so much wisdom, morality, and even holiness in her advice.

LEARNING TO LIVE WITHOUT A MAN

Michelle

Let's say it all together: "Mand-aid!" Yep, I love it. This con-cept is so true and so definitely me. And allow me to be bold and say that most of you can probably relate. I think there is something so normal about experiencing a devastating loss and wanting to replace what we've lost. Yet when we do it prematurely before our hearts are ready to experience it, like Connie said, we experience greater pain, further heart wounds, and set ourselves up for more loss.

Some of you will heed this advice, and some will have to experience the burn before realizing your heart is fragile and not yet ready to forge full speed ahead. We are here for you, and our hope is to share with you wisdom from mistakes made and keep you on that journey back to wholeness and a healthy you.

I remember Connie saying to me, "Yeah, Michelle, I know God is with me, but I just wanna feel some skin." I love how she tells it like it is. We all want to feel someone close, someone who will hold us and tell us it's all going to be okay. I wish someone would have been there to help navigate the road more clearly for me, and I most definitely wish I would have had a book that had authors who had gone before me and could give me advice from experience.

Like Connie, I was an emotional mess after my divorce. You don't go through open-heart surgery without major setbacks and emotional trauma. I don't think most of us realize just how traumatic divorce really is. I had enough sense in me not to go out and do an all-out manhunt looking for mand-aids.

Some of it is just plain validation. You need someone to tell you you're okay and to make you feel okay. Yet you are too weary, too broken, and too out of your mind to actually make good decisions about anything in the process, much less a sexual relationship. You remember the Mel Gibson movie *What Women Want*? Well, what if we could really get in the mind of a man and know their thoughts? I think most of us would be surprised.

While we women are thinking, *Hold me, love me, fill me,* men are thinking, *Give me, take care of me, don't talk to me too much.*

I am not going to pretend to know the minds of men, but I will say the minds of men and the minds of women after divorce are not too far apart. They both want the same thing, they both need to be validated, and they both need, need, need. So you have two very unhealthy, self-focused, needy, desperate people; what do you think you are going to get? Definitely not a successful, loving relationship built on trust, love, and serving each other.

Picture this: Your ship has gone down in the middle of the ocean, and not only have you jumped ship, but you also have only one thing to keep you alive, a little buoy that the sunken ship left behind. You're both reaching for the buoy and holding on to it for dear life because you're both drowning. Ultimately you end up pushing each other into the water instead of bringing each other to safety. Why? Because wounded people, while they desperately need love, are not yet ready to receive it.

People who are hurting and wounded can't let you in their territory without feeling they can totally trust you. My mom was speaking at an event, and afterward when it was time to pray for everyone, a girl came forward to be prayed for. We are a hugging family, and when my mom finished praying and went to hug the girl, the girl stepped back. My mom, being from a family history of abuse, immediately knew this girl could not be hugged. A few weeks later the girl sent my mom a letter telling of her hurt, abuse, and pain and then signed it, "The girl who could not be hugged."

When you are coming out of divorce, you have many wounds. You didn't fall and scrape your knee; you were in a deadly car accident and are barely holding on for life. You don't just bounce back from the trauma; you slowly work your way back into life at a pace that makes sense and doesn't cause you further injury.

The term *mand-aid* is perfect because that is simply what it is, a temporary solution to an injury that needs much more than a bandage. You are in need of some serious heart surgery that will help you begin the process of healing. I didn't even wait to sign the dotted line on my divorce before I was in therapy working with a counselor to sort through the mess my mind and heart was in.

I didn't focus on what my former spouse's issues were; I desired to find out what mine were and why I kept choosing the same kind of person over and over again. When you are in your lowest place, you are attracted to people in that same place. To get right back in the dating game so you can medicate your pain is not healing yourself long term. It's just a temporary fix. Like Connie said, we want to be honest with you about our lives so you can know we relate to where you are.

As I said earlier, within months of my divorce, well-meaning people tried to set me up and get me back out there. I don't think people like seeing others alone and in pain. My heart was to please the Lord, to make sure I did things right. I definitely didn't want to date a lot of guys and just sleep around. I'm a one-man kind of gal and loved being married, so all I could think about was getting married again. I felt I would not be whole again with the hole that was left in my heart. It was like someone had cut off my arm, and I needed to find the replacement before I could function again. I wanted so much to believe God would bring me a man not just for me but for my children. With four kids under the age of ten, I felt extremely lost and afraid. I had no idea how I would take care of these four precious kids, and my child support didn't begin to cover the expenses. Can you relate? The thought of taking care of them alone was petrifying and overwhelming for me.

I remember vividly the day I sat in my counselor's office and said, "I cannot live without a sexual relationship." He calmly looked at me and responded, "Yes, you can." What I was really saying is, "I need love. I need, I need, I need someone next to me to fall asleep with and share my day and help me carry the weight of all that is on my plate" . . . and it was a lot. "I need someone to share life success with. I need someone to give me what only God can truly give, abundant, grace-filled love. I can't live without that." But what my wise counselor was saying is, "With God all things are possible—you can and will live without this, and God will sustain you."

I was in counseling with him for several years, and I will never forget the day I sat in his office and was able to say, "You were right. I can live without a man, and I have, and I am happy." Wow! That was such a huge accomplishment coming from a person who had never in her life been without a man. From the time I was sixteen and started to date I went from one serious relationship to another. The only break I had was right before I met my former spouse. I had come into a relationship with Christ and had taken a break from men and relationships. It had been about eight months when I met him. I didn't know what it meant to be alone even then. My dream was to be married and have kids, and when I met my former husband, I could not have been happier or felt more settled.

We don't really change much as women. We desire Prince Charming, even when we know our wholeness comes from the Lord. What changes is a man is no longer an idol, but an added bonus to the fulfillment and peace we already feel deep inside. Do you feel that peace? Do you feel whole without a man in your life?

The sexual relationship is a way for women to feel that wholeness for a moment, but what happens when he leaves the next morning? The emptiness is more painful, and the insecurity that comes as a result can cause major conflict in a relationship. You don't feel secure when you are in a sexual relationship with a man you are not married to simply because you are not secure in any way. When you enter into a marriage covenant, you at least know you have an agreement together. He can't just walk out the next day and leave you. There is a comfort knowing you mean enough to the other person for him to give his word before God and men and to honor you in a way that is pleasing to God.

As women we dream of a man who can be all things to us. He will be good looking, talk to us about our emotions, go shopping with us, father our children, sweep us off our feet, make passionate love to us, and go out and work all day to provide for us and make us feel safe. It's a tall order, but it's close to what most women want.

What I didn't realize after my divorce was that I definitely was not in my right mind to discern someone healthy who would love me and be great to my kids. After divorce, more than any time in your life, you are in a place where it is easy to be duped, and there are many men out there who are not who they say they are.

I had my share of bad relationships after my divorce. Each one taught me something different, but the most important thing I realized is no one but God could fill the void. I truly loved my kids' father, and it would be years before I would feel even close to emotionally healthy again. You don't walk away from fifteen years of history with someone and feel fine.

It's easy to get into what I call "situational theology." Divorce catapulted me into a place where I felt disappointed with God and His principles, and being in a place of despair can sometimes lead to stinking thinking, where we rationalize God's truth in His Word to fit our lifestyle at the time. We start making decisions our way and on our terms and don't consult God on the everyday decisions that can steer our lives in one direction or the next, and we pay no attention to the consequences that will come as a result of us being behind the wheel.

Sex can be one of those decisions we tend to rationalize away. Hey, this is our situation, and we can't help it, so we can make choices based on that, right? Wrong! I had a Christian worship leader actually say to me, "Michelle, we are adults, and sex is a necessity." I just gently told him if you are going to have a sexual relationship and sin, then do it, but don't say God is okay with it because He isn't, and believing that is a lie.

I tell my kids, "If you do something wrong, then kick your own butt. Don't leave it up to God to have to do it for you." It's easy to rationalize sin, even to blame God for your sin because you are now divorced. When we begin to get confused about what truth really is, we can always go back to God's Word and see what He says about sexual immorality. However, let's take it a step further.

One thing I tell my kids is to look at the why factor. *Why* does God not want us to have a sexual relationship outside of marriage? I spoke to a girl recently who is not a believer, and she had just gone on a first date with a guy. As we talked I advised her to take it slow physically, to avoid a physical relationship with someone unless she feels she is going to marry the guy. She laughed and said, "It's too late for that. I had a need to fill, and I filled it." But did she? Did she really wake up the next day and feel whole and satisfied?

As we talked she shared with me how she had no idea if

this guy wanted to see her again. I could tell she was concerned about it. Basically it was a temporary fix to a longing in her soul that definitely could not be filled by one night of sex. We are not mechanical beings. We have a soul and a heart and hopefully a conscience. She went on to justify her actions by telling me how men have sex whenever they want and think nothing of it, so why couldn't she? As she shared, I could hear the insecurity in her voice, the sense of hopefulness that he would call and he would care about her, love her, and show interest in her. She gave a part of her soul to someone who may never call her again and left absolutely no mystery to herself. Why would he want to seek her out? For more sex? Would you want someone to want you for that reason alone? When we give ourselves away so easily, we leave absolutely no reason for a man to pursue us. Men are characters of pursuit. They like the game. They are hunters. When they have caught their game and you leave them no reason to hunt or to desire to get to know you on a level they would fall in love with you for, they have no reason to continue. How many times have we seen it in movies: a woman brokenhearted because the guy never calls? Ladies, hello?

What do you value? Do you value the physical relationship between a man and a woman, or is it simply something you need to add to your to-do list to get done in a week? Had sex . . . check. You then become something on his to-do list instead of someone he values, wants, and desires to pursue.

Do you value yourself? Do you think the man this girl slept with truly values her? Is this a great way to start a relationship with someone you may want to marry? To think someone can so easily give it away without any regard to the consequences is common, and it's due to perspective. The way we look at sex and what God created to be an intimate union between a man and a woman who are in covenant together has everything to do with the decisions we make about sex.

I consider myself a progressive thinker, an adult, a woman with needs. Yet if I just go out and take what I want in the moment or even in a long-term relationship, without considering what God says in His Word, I am saying that I know more than God when it comes to what is best for me.

I wish I could tell you it was easy. Just don't have sex unless you're married. No problem. Unfortunately, this is not the case. In fact, the whole sexual factor was a huge part of a decision I made to jump into a new relationship, and it had serious consequences—not just for me, but for my kids.

Like some of you, after being married for a long time, I had no idea how to date. In fact, the last thing I wanted to do, desired to do, was date. I loved being married and never dreamed I'd find myself single in my thirties. Even though I was disappointed with God, I still wanted to please Him.

So when Prince Charming came and swept me and the kids off our feet, buying us gifts, showering me with the praise I hadn't had in so long, praying with me, and having the appearance of a man who loved God with his whole heart, I bought it hook, line, and sinker. Unfortunately, this man turned out to be a counterfeit who was not only abusive but had an addiction to pornography.

I thought I had done the due diligence needed, but instead I seem to have talked to all the wrong people. It was only later that many of the people I needed to talk to, from ex-wives to ex-girlfriends in his life, came to me and shared their stories of abuse and heartbreak.

What I could not grasp was how a man who spoke God's Word like no other I had met and prayed what I thought were sincere prayers of care for me could turn around and wrap his hands around my neck and threaten to kill me for something trivial.

I went away to my mom's retreat center in Texas to pray and seek the Lord on what I should do. It's my haven and place of solitude in times when I need answers—and I needed answers badly. I didn't want another breakup in my life, but I realized this man was a threat to me and to my children. My babies, who had already been through so much, had now been hurt by this person I had allowed into my life. I cannot even begin to tell you my regret and heartbreak over the time spent with him.

He had pulled the God card. It's so easy to fall for, and boy did I. He seemed so spiritual, and as we grew in our relationship, I became more and more confused. He did ministry, he said all the right things, and people thought he was great; but behind the scenes he was an abuser and a sex addict. I had never encountered such deception, so it took me some time to sort it through.

While at my mom's, I was awakened in the middle of the night, and out of nowhere this verse kept coming to me over and over again: "If I have a faith that can move mountains, but do not have love, I am nothing" (1 Corinthians 13:2).

He had been through many things in his life and had shared with me his own journey of abuse. He was void of love—not just for me, but for himself. When a person hates himself, he cannot love anyone else or give love to anyone else. My being with someone who didn't value me was also an act of self-hatred. How could I love and give love to someone when I didn't even value myself and believe I was worth something?

I had wanted so badly to do things in a way that would honor

God, most specifically in the area of a physical relationship, and I was looking for the perfect Christian guy. It's so easy to get duped here, ladies. Be careful with this. Don't rush into a relationship or a marriage just because someone tells you he is a Christian and uses all the right lingo. Make sure you spend time getting to know him to find out if his actions line up with his words. I wanted so much to fill the hole in my heart, the void and deep, dark canyon in my soul, and somehow thought a man would fix everything. I wanted to believe so badly, I think I would have believed anything. Can you relate?

Have you had these thoughts: *Who will ever want me? Who will ever love me and my children again?* These questions haunted me daily. It had been only six months out of my divorce, and I was truly a wreck on every level due to the emotional roller coaster in the marriage to my kids' father, yet at the time I didn't see or realize my condition. All I knew was I needed help, and the thought of being a single mom to four kids was so overwhelming it was at times almost debilitating. The wounds and heart bruises from the marriage to my kids' father never had a chance to heal, and another relationship of any kind in the state I was in would most likely be destined to fail.

Prince Charming was not who he said he was. I know some of you reading this can totally relate. You, too, have been duped with a counterfeit relationship. I listened recently to a friend who has had the same history of choosing men who were abusive. Here she was coming out of an abusive relationship again, and as she talked, she said something so important for those who find themselves time and time again with men who do not value them. "Why do these men keep using and abusing me?" She was placing all the blame on the abusers and the men who had hurt her. I gently said to her, "Sweet girl, you don't value yourself." This doesn't mean she deserved the abuse by any means. Most definitely not. But men who abuse look for vulnerable and weak women who have low self-esteem. We have to do the work it takes to get ourselves to a healthy place, or we will keep choosing the same person over and over again.

I grew up in abuse and was attracted to what was familiar to me. My kids' father never physically abused me, but he was emotionally detached and not present. His choice to end our marriage was one he later came back to say he regretted, but by that time I was not only a different person but also emotionally in a more whole and healthy place, and choosing to be back in a marriage with him would be choosing not to value myself.

For years after the divorce I didn't value myself and chose men who didn't value me. After ending the relationship with Prince Charming, who abused me, I made the decision to understand why. For the next seven years, I took the time I should have taken right after my divorce to heal, get new perspective, and seek the Lord. I pursued my emotional health and worked on me. I wanted to understand why I kept choosing the same type of men who didn't value me.

I learned some important things not only about myself but also about these men. They don't value themselves and cannot give love due to the lack of love they have for themselves. Needless to say, after much counsel and time spent alone with the Lord, I began to pick up the pieces to my broken life.

It is certainly not easy to talk about my journey. In fact, I have purposely not talked about it for such a long time due to the darkness, pain, and shame of it all, and yet God's restorative and gentle way of leading us back on the right path is why I am sharing this with you. If I share only my successes and my joy, and skip the journey of how I arrived to where I am today, what purpose would it serve? Connie and I chose to write on divorce because we know the devastation and fallout of it, and we desire to share the road of good choices that we feel will begin to lead you on the journey to wholeness and a happy, healthy, new you.

You don't have to be with an abuser to be with the wrong guy. Whatever you do, don't settle; don't get married again to be married, especially because you feel you need a sexual relationship. The hardships of being single don't compare to the loneliness and despair of a bad marriage. I could have been married again long before I made the choice to be married. My years of singleness were not easy. I was cautious more than ever, and those relationships had temporarily destroyed my faith in men. The last thing I wanted was to be married again or for that matter even date.

During my single years, I did meet a man who restored my overall faith in men. I actually thought we would marry eventually, but something inside me kept saying no. It's easy to come out of bad relationships and then meet someone who is good to you, and in comparing him to past relationships he seems perfect. However, is he the person you are supposed to spend the rest of your life with? We spent a long time going back and forth, constantly struggling with the sexual issue, but still really seeking God as to whether we should be together long term.

While he was a great man, I knew our marriage would be settling instead of waiting on what God had for me. Could I trust God? Would I trust Him? I had to come to terms with the reality that I may never marry again. Was I okay with that? It was the hardest decision. As single women, we can grapple with this time and time again. It's hard to be single and continue to trust God with your life. This guy was a great man, a great dad, and my kids loved him, but he was not for me. To choose being alone over being with someone who was so good to me and treated me better than any man I ever had was not easy. In fact, it was one of the hardest decisions I have ever made, but I felt I was choosing God's obedience for my life over my own will.

If God knows me so well and knows the deepest part of me in every way, why wouldn't He want me to choose the best for me? Why wouldn't I trust Him then to bring me my husband should He choose to? I was tired of my choices and was ready for God's choices for my life, whatever that looked like.

Some of you are having to make decisions about relationships, and I would ask yourself this question: "Am I with this person because I believe we are supposed to be together, and I am truly called to be this person's life partner in a marriage, or am I with him because he is filling a need, and I just don't want to be alone?"

During my long-term relationship with this good guy, I pursued my emotional health and began not only to get strong but also to value myself for the first time ever. I was not going to settle for anything less than God's greatest purpose and plan for my life. Not only did that mean I would have to wait on Him, but it meant surrendering the fact I may never marry again. I was ready. God was wooing my heart and filling me up with His abundant love.

I felt I was in the desert during this time with no water and no place to go, allowing my fleshly desires to be burned out of me completely. It was not easy. I felt so alone—yet that is exactly where He wanted me so He could love on me, so He could show me what true love is, and so that He alone would be my provider.

You may be thinking, *Yeah, yeah, Michelle, whatever. How am*

I supposed to just trust God with my life, my finances, my heart, my sexual desires? It's tough being a single mom, and I'm supposed to leave these things all up to Him?

I know. I understand how hard it is, but for us to have God's best and not settle for the "good" we have to get to the place where we surrender our sexual needs, our financial needs, and our emotional needs to Him and entrust our lives to Him. It was a long journey for me, but I am so thankful for it. I had to deal with my emotional junk to get to the place God was able to finally take the wheel and get me on the right road again. I am grateful for the journey, as painful as it was. I've never been one to walk alone, and I realized that I wasn't ever actually alone; He truly was there for me on every level.

The process of crushing my own determination was the burning down of me and the building up of Him in my life. It was amazing to get to the place where I'd walk in a room and feel whole instead of feeling like a half person.

During the time right before I met Michael, my amazing husband, I had come to realize dating wasn't an option, at least traditional dating as we know it. I set a lot of boundaries, which included not having a physical relationship, period. No kissing on first dates, no going to each other's homes or even driving in the car together. I know it sounds extreme, but even in our healthiest state we are still extremely vulnerable.

I set the same rules and boundaries for my teenage daughter, who has been in a relationship for a while. I am extremely proud of how she doesn't take for granted her own ability to be strong. We are human, and that's why more than ever we have to set those boundaries.

God created us to feel, to love, to express love and emotion, and to give ourselves completely to someone within the context of marriage.

So back to why. "Why Wait" is a campaign for young girls to stay pure and keep their virginity, and the same holds true for us. Do you really want to give a part of yourself to someone over and over and over again only to have him take a piece of you? Don't you know God thinks so highly of us He created those boundaries for us? When we meet the man of our dreams, the man we want and desire to give ourselves totally to, how do we think we will feel when we have been with so many different people? Do you think we are so without feeling we can just sleep with someone and come away unscathed? Will our judgment not be clouded? What advice would you give your virgin self at thirteen, fourteen, fifteen?

Girl, valuing yourself, respecting yourself, will feel great, and if a man can't respect that, then as Connie says, hit Delete. More on valuing and respecting yourself in chapter 7.

YOU and Sex Thoughts

We hope by sharing our own situations you might be able to identify with one or both of us in some way. We know it's a natural progression to want to go to another level, a deeper level with someone you're dating and very attracted to. It's hard to put the kibosh on something that is such a natural instinct. If you've crossed the line with one or more men since your divorce, we don't want to throw the book at you.

We do not want you to live in guilt and condemnation. We would challenge you to ask yourself a few poignant questions about the depth of your relationship with God. How committed is your relationship? Is it a Sunday thing or is it a life commitment? If you've fallen in love with God, then you'll want to please Him more, just as you would that earthly person you love. Where do your priorities lie?

We encourage you to read the Scriptures regarding this topic and ask the Holy Spirit to speak to your heart. Then take the time to listen to what He has to say. Ask for a fresh revelation of where He's calling you to be and what He's calling you to do. Is He just being cruel? Or is He trying to protect you? Would He ask you to do something that is utterly impossible? Is He asking you to lay it down for the rest of your life or until the right person comes along that you know He wants you to spend the rest of your life with? How would you advise your children, if you have them, about sex outside of marriage? These are just a few questions to ponder before you "do da job."

YOU and Sex Actions

- How deep is your relationship with Jesus? Is it a heart commitment that takes precedence over everything else? Do you listen to the leading of the Holy Spirit? He will direct your thoughts regarding this topic.
- When you have a sexual relationship with a man, you are leaving a piece of yourself with him, thus creating a soul tie. Wouldn't you rather give yourself to the right man that God has for you at the right time instead of leaving fragments of yourself with other men? Take

some time to pray and ask the Lord to forgive you for these soul ties and to wash you clean of your sin. Ask the Lord to show you ways to keep yourself from falling into a sexual relationship again, and write down what comes to mind. Also, think of some practical ways you can keep yourself pure.

- How would you advise your children, a loved one, or dear friend about sex outside of marriage?
- You can't hide anything from God. Be honest with your feelings about this topic, and talk to Him about it. He'll help you deal with it.
- How do you see yourself when it comes to your value? Do you feel you are respecting yourself and protecting your possible future marriage relationship?

YOU and Sex Prayer

Lord, I don't understand Your ways and thoughts. But I know that I can trust You to help me do all You have called me to do. My goal and heart's desire is to please You with my life. You would not call me to do anything that was out of the realm of possibility. Help me make good and right choices for my good and the good of others. As Your bride, I pray that if it is Your will for me to remarry, that You will give me the willpower to wait for the right man who is to be my husband. Your Word says that I can do all things through You. I know that my help comes from You. It is in the name of Jesus I pray with thanksgiving, amen.

six

YOU AND MONEY

We love the scene in *Jerry Maguire* when Tom Cruise and Cuba Gooding Jr. practically rap passionately back and forth, "Show me the money, show me the money!" Like Jerry Maguire, whose passion has run out due to the lack of authenticity in his working relationships, we, too, can easily find ourselves basing major life decisions simply on money. Whether it is due to the lack of it or an overflow of it, money is to be considered when it comes to marriage, and especially marriages that involve kids.

We've all heard the horror stories. We've seen the tears of women who have fallen prey in their vulnerability to men who legally robbed them of a large amount of money. Sometimes their entire life savings. Then there are those women who financially support men for fear of being alone. Honestly, that's not far off from prostitution.

Then there are women who have been home for many years taking care of the home and the children. You know, keeping the old, traditional family values. Pretty much like how it was a generation or two ago. Many of these women stayed home and put off their own careers for the sake of taking care of the home and family, but to support their mates as they went to school and furthered their education leading to a great job. And now they find themselves alone with no skills. They don't know where to start and figure it'll take a lifetime before they'll be able to live the life they were accustomed to when they were married. So they rush right out to look for another mate. And the first qualification they're looking for is someone who has deep pockets. Someone who will provide for them. You've heard the old saying, "Marry the first time for love and the second time for money."

And then there are those women who stay in abusive relationships because their husbands have a lot of money and shower them with all the material goods they could ever hope for. The marriage is empty, so they try to find their comfort in a beautiful home, jewelry, clothes, plastic surgery, and endless hours at the spa. But there's never enough stuff to fill the hole in their lives.

Money . . . we try not to make it so important, yet somehow it ranks high on the list of what we're looking for in a partner. But the way a person handles money is very telling about his character and integrity. For example, let's say you're on a date with a guy and when he pays for the ice cream, the young clerk behind the counter accidentally gives him twenty dollars in excess change. Your date doesn't flinch and rejoices in his good fortune. What does that tell you about him?

We have seen a lot of capable, kind, and intelligent women do some pretty dumb things when it comes to money and men. We will share something from our own stories on what we've learned about this topic.

LEARNING TO MANAGE MONEY

Connie

When I found myself going through a divorce a decade ago, I was living the traditional family values lifestyle. My husband was the primary breadwinner. I dabbled in recording session work and worked part-time for a few years at the local radio station doing the morning show. Thankfully, I had skills and things I enjoyed doing; however, I never managed our money. My husband made far more than I did, and his area of expertise was finance, so I let him handle all our finances. I didn't know anything about our insurance policies, taxes, savings, or investments. I had no idea who our agents or bankers were. That was not because he kept it from me; it's because I didn't care. Money management wasn't my thing, and I assumed he'd take care of it forever. Bad move. Now I encourage all women to learn about handling money, and if they're married, to be knowledgeable and active in making the decisions about banking, investments, purchases, insurance policies, and anything else related to your finances. My husband was the obvious choice for being the money handler, but I was unwise not to know what was going on. When he left, it was another problem added to all the pain and grief I felt while going through divorce. Now I also had to learn about money.

If you are divorced, and you haven't worked outside the home for some time, you will have to start with making a budget. After taking alimony and/or child support into consideration, write out a monthly budget, and see where you stand and how much, if any, you fall short. If you don't know how to do a budget, there are several great books out there to help you. I would definitely recommend all the Dave Ramsey books. *Financial Peace* and *The*

Total Money Makeover are great resources.[1] If you can attend Financial Peace University, it would be well worth it for you. (Go to www.DaveRamsey.com and click on "classes," which will take you to the "Financial Peace University" link.) You'll come away knowing a great deal more about money and how to handle it.

I know that when you're strapped for cash, the last thing you want to think about is giving. This is the only place in the Bible where God challenges us to test Him. "'Bring all the tithes into the storehouse, that there may be food in My house, and try Me now in this,' says the LORD of hosts. 'If I will not open for you the windows of heaven and pour out for you such blessing that there will not be room enough to receive it'" (Malachi 3:10 NKJV). Even if it's hard to write that tithe check, I encourage you to do it and see what God will do. He is your provider. If you have children, remember to teach them the principles of giving, saving, and buying wisely. And the earlier, the better.

Once you do your budget, then you need to start exploring ways to cover your expenses if they aren't already. There are lots of ways to generate cash. One way is to have a garage sale or start selling things on Craigslist or eBay. The important thing is to spend less money than you make. I know lots of single moms who shop at thrift shops, flea markets, consignment shops, and garage sales. They spend very little and come home with a lot.

Spend some time thinking about what interests you and makes you feel good about yourself. If you find something you love and something you're good at, try to form a business involving your passion. All you need is one client to start the ball rolling, and then build on that. You can promote your business or services on social media and create your own website. In the interim, while growing your business, you will probably have to take some other job to generate cash until your dream job grows enough. Studies have shown that if you spend a couple hours a week investing in the job you want to have, eventually you'll have it. Before long, after all your hard work and perseverance, you will have developed a career you love, and you will be generating enough income to quit the other job. And all the time invested will have been worth it.

There are perks to being employed by someone else and perks to being self-employed. Just like there is the downside in both scenarios. That's the way it is with all things in life. There is never a perfect situation. So make sure you do the thing that's going to work for you and give you the fewest headaches. In other words, make sure the positives outweigh the negatives.

I've always said that when choosing a mate, it's important to connect with him on a spiritual, emotional, intellectual, and financial level. Why financial? Because the way you view money and how to handle it should be the same with both parties. Otherwise, you're headed for disaster. I'll go a step further and say that it's probably important the second time around for you and your husband to be in the same ballpark as far as income and debt ratio. Hopefully, neither of you will have much debt, except for your home and/or cars, and I think it is best if you are in the same general vicinity as far as income. Some people will not agree with that. It's a matter of preference and just my opinion that it will work better for you in the long run to have similar financial situations. Did I do that in one of the serious relationships I was in? No. I didn't form that opinion until my engagement with Rick bombed big time. (I will tell you about our relationship in the next chapter.)

Let's visit the idea of a prenuptial agreement. I will mention

Dave Ramsey again and say that he doesn't believe in them at all. Some think prenups show a lack of trust. Let's come up with a couple of fictitious scenarios to help you look at this in a different light:

Scenario 1: You're a divorced woman in your forties. Your ex-husband was not wealthy but left you with an alimony and/or child support package that is helpful. You don't have a lot of assets. You work at a boutique, and you're engaged to be married to a professional man who does very well. He doesn't have much debt and seems to be very responsible with money. Five years later the marriage dissolves. You've split half the assets, and now you're in your mid- to late forties with several years left to work—meaning you have fifteen-plus years of earning power ahead of you. Do you wish you'd had a prenup? We'll be your counselor and ask you, "What do you think?"

Scenario 2: You're in your mid-fifties. You've been divorced for a while. Your ex left you with a nice settlement. You've saved and invested wisely. Your parents are deceased and left you with a decent inheritance. You work at the same boutique, and you live a comfortable lifestyle. You're engaged to be married to a man who has some debt and is not doing quite as well as you are financially, but he enjoys his work and brings in a steady paycheck. The marriage dissolves five years later, and he walks out with half of your inheritance and investment savings from your previous marriage. You're now pushing sixty, you're getting closer to retirement age, and you're still working at the boutique with not a lot of earning power ahead of you. Do you wish you'd had a prenup? What do you think?

We wish everything in life could be cut-and-dried, black-and-white. Some things are and some things aren't. Of course we should implicitly trust our husbands or the man we intend to marry. But I would've bet a million dollars plus my left lung and even the farm that my husband never would have left me. That's how secure I thought our marriage was. It was a complete shock to me when it ended.

Prenup or not? Only you can decide.

One last thing about money. If you were married to your spouse for ten years and you don't remarry, you are entitled to the spousal benefits on his Social Security package. However, you cannot take your benefits and his . . . only one. So, obviously, you'd want to choose the one that is higher. I've recently heard that if you remarry after sixty years of age, you are still entitled to your spousal benefits from your ex. To be sure, check with your Social Security office.

Michelle

I was not dependent on a man for money until I married my kids' father. His job allowed me to stay home and take care of the kids, something I am very thankful for. When my youngest son was only three, I began to do different things that generated some income. This was quite the change in our marriage, and I believe a bit of a challenge for my kids' dad. However, if I had not gone down that track, I can't imagine what I would have done after our divorce.

Like many of you, I had no idea I'd be divorced, and I definitely didn't have a savings account on the side just in case. Once the divorce was final, I had to figure out how to manage my life on the small child support I was being given and whatever income I could make. It wasn't easy with four children, which is one of the reasons I was drawn into a relationship right after my divorce. I loved him, but I was also thinking of the long-term help it would bring. What I didn't know was he was riddled with debt and, since I actually made more money than he did, he was expecting me to eventually pay his off. I'll never forget the phone conversation with my mom when I told her he had called me from work one afternoon saying he'd never be happy until I had paid off his debt. Yes, you heard me right. Connie had the same experience with a man she was engaged to briefly.

When you have kids, your children are your responsibility. Life is no longer just about you. It's important to realize this when making the decision to date someone. Be careful and set up the boundaries around your finances. In your desperation to love and be loved, you may be persuaded to buy your happiness, but anyone who would ask that of you is a counterfeit and will most likely burn you over time. No man who loves a woman would ask her to take money she needs to provide for her children and use it on him. Beware of any man who asks you to financially help him or provide for him.

I have yet to meet a divorced woman who comes out of the marriage financially better off. When you are creating two households, the budget you have always worked with is suddenly cut in half, and at the same time no one wants to give or budge on what they need or want. The financial dilemma begins, and it is a recipe for disaster. I was broken down and such a wreck over my divorce that in the process of dividing up assets and determining child support, I totally left it up to him and honestly didn't have the strength to even care. I was so broken by his decision and what he was doing that I could not even fathom the idea of going to court and hashing through the nightmare of facing him to tear apart our lives in front of complete strangers. Thankfully he is a good person overall and did things pretty fairly. I've never had to take him back to court or argue about something major. We work together well in the best interest of the kids.

However, this is not the case for most of the divorced women I know. They have had to go to court more than once, and there is an ongoing war over finances. Regardless of your situation, put a financial plan in place ASAP.

Remember, you are now the head of your household. There is no time for weak knees or a weak stomach; you have to be tough and take care of you and those babies. Some of you may have tears even as you read this. I know it's not easy. Lay your burden at the cross for Jesus to bear. It is not for you to carry. He will see you through.

I remember lying in bed one night toward the end of my marriage, thinking, *What will I do financially? How will I take care of these kids and myself? What is the plan, Lord?* I distinctly remember sensing God whisper, *Michelle, I am the plan. Put your faith and your trust in Me, and I will see you through.* And He has. Through thick and thin, good times and bad, God has seen us through, and we are all better for it, more appreciative, and wiser.

God is the plan, but He says to us to make our plans and then allow for Him to change them if He needs to. "Commit your actions to the LORD, and your plans will succeed" (Proverbs 16:3 NLT). Make your plans and then commit them to the Lord.

As you sort through the mess of your divorce, think through a plan for the well-being of your family. What is the best route that will allow you to be there for the kids and yet make the money you need to provide for them? You may need a two-year plan to go to school. I know many divorced women who have gone back to school. It may require you to live conservatively for a couple of years, but think about the long-term advantages. Whatever your plan consists of, you can do it. Don't allow doubt, discouragement, or low self-esteem to keep you from doing what you need to do for your family. It's amazing what you can do and what ideas have been products of sheer desperation. How many success stories have you heard about someone who was living in an apartment, on her last dime, and suddenly came up with an idea that made her a success?

As an entrepreneur and a life coach, my advice is to make sure you do something in your range of talent. If you are great with people, think of everything you could do with people, such as customer service, communications, public relations, and sales. If you are great with numbers, think of what you could do to help people grow their revenues, or how you could be of help with their accounting. You need some experience to get you the next opportunity, so even if you have to volunteer to show someone you are good at what you do, then do it. You just need someone to believe in you and your talent to get you started on a path of success.

Here is a quick checklist for you to consider when looking for work:

1. Think everyone you know who might be able to help you start a new career by allowing you to do some things on the side for them.
2. Make a list of every opportunity you think would line up with your talent and passion, and make a plan to get you there.
3. This is a time to ask for help. Don't be afraid to get a mentor who can help you walk through ideas.

4. The best bosses are usually women who will understand you're a single mom. Get in a single moms' group, and find women for whom you may be able to work who will understand if you need to run out and get the kids or be home early for an event.

5. Insurance is a must. If you have a job without insurance benefits, work part-time at Starbucks or a company that offers insurance to part-time employees.

6. Don't be afraid to try a new career or start a career. Depending on getting married again for financial security is a huge mistake. Be independent so financial desperation doesn't determine your next relationship.

In the past you may have left the finances up to your husband. Now you are single, and the finances are up to you. Don't let money intimidate you, but if handling the finances is not something you do well, get some help. While I was able to bring in enough income, I was not great at managing it, especially when I was in survival mode. If you are struggling in this area, find a financial adviser you can trust to help you with some long-term planning. Make sure you do your due diligence and that he or she is trustworthy. I would also recommend you get educated on financial investments and other aspects of financial assistance.

A lot of moms have to temporarily file for state assistance and state insurance. While we are not promoting depending on the government long term, we are suggesting if your kids' livelihood depends on it, don't be afraid to get help temporarily until you are back on your feet.

One issue I have seen a lot of divorced parents struggle

with is giving guilt money or gifts to their children. None of us desired to be divorced or wanted this for our kids. However, no amount of money or gifts can make up for the loss, and they actually end up being more damaging than helpful. What would we be teaching them anyway? Just like we don't need to self-medicate on material things, we don't need to teach our kids to. What they need is your love and attention more than anything. If you want to invest in something, invest in their emotional and mental well-being by getting them in a support group with kids their age or some kind of therapy specifically for kids.

Most divorced women are not able to leave their marriages without the baggage of debt in tow. There are those few fortunate ones who are well taken care of and don't have to worry about finances, but for most of us, this is not the case. Debt can be a real stress point and may seem overwhelming at times. The main thing to think about here is creating a plan for how you intend to get rid of it over a period of time. Don't look at how much you owe, just look at your plan, and every month whittle the debt down a little at a time. Pretty soon what seemed like a mountain is now a small hill.

I would contact those you owe money to and let them know your status. Some will more than accommodate you. I had to borrow some funds to get a fresh start and used the money I received from the payoff of my home to pay the debt. When we have a plan in place, it relieves us from thinking constantly about the mountain of debt on our plates. Write it all down, and focus on your budget monthly. Whatever you do, don't make big debt decisions when you are just coming out of your divorce.

YOU and Money Thoughts

The most important point of this chapter is to encourage you to learn how to be responsible for yourself. Learn the money basics, and be wise. Don't ever give in to a man asking you for money or even a loan. This is a red flag, and it's huge and waving furiously. Don't buy in to any sad stories. Don't ever discuss your personal financial information with someone you're dating. On the other hand, if you're dating someone seriously and you're looking at spending your lives together, then you will need to know everything about your intended other's financial picture, and he has every right to know about yours. We suggest a good dose of premarital counseling before doing that. But don't be buying property or opening joint bank accounts with anybody until you've both said "I do." We also encourage you to change your banking passwords often to prevent identity theft.

Don't count on finding a husband to be your meal ticket. Although it would be wonderful if we all had helpmates who could assist with our money issues, the reality is this: maybe you will remarry, and maybe you won't. I know many of you don't want to hear that. That's why it's important for you to find something you can do to support yourself. Learn about retirement savings. Meet with a financial planner. If you get the money thing down, you will be much less stressed. Life is stressful enough without always having to worry about paying your bills.

And last but not least, always remember that God is your provider. Remember His promise. He makes a way when it seems as though there is no way. And that's one thing you can bank on.

YOU and Money Actions

1. Don't ever give or loan money to a man you are dating.
2. Don't open up a bank account, secure a credit card, or buy a car or property with a man who is not your spouse.
3. Work toward your dream job. Try to earn money doing something you enjoy that matches your passions.
4. Learn the basics of money—how to save, invest, give, and spend wisely.
5. Secure life insurance, disability income, and health insurance.
6. Finally, it doesn't matter how old you are. Please create a will. There are websites that can help you create one.

YOU and Money Prayer

Father, help me be a good steward with my finances. Give me wisdom concerning saving, giving, and spending wisely. Help me be a responsible person regarding that which You've given me. Increase my lot, Lord. Open up the windows of heaven, and pour out a financial blessing in accordance with Your Word to help me do well, further Your kingdom, and bless others. Provide work for me that makes my heart sing,

Lord. Help me cross the right paths of others who may help me obtain my dream job. I thank You that You order my steps. Lead me and guide me to always remain on the right path and walk in Your ways. It's in Jesus' name I pray, amen.

seven

YOU AND RESPECT

If there is any one chapter outside of the one on forgiveness that we want you to get, it's this one. Oh, how easy it is to lose respect for yourself, especially after a divorce. We feel we've been "marked" as women who couldn't go the distance. As a result, we sell ourselves short of God's best to settle for hand-me-down seconds because we weren't willing to patiently walk through the process necessary to protect our hearts, our children, our assets, and most of all, our lives. It's called settling. We know all about this because we were there and had to learn the hard way.

We firmly believe that if you don't take the time needed to heal from your divorce or other broken relationships, you will continue to go down the same path repeatedly, and this vicious cycle will be a part of your life forever. Going through some downtime after divorce, letting the dust settle, and getting professional counseling are the most important steps to take before diving into another relationship. Most people are not willing to put in the time and effort needed to obtain healing. Everybody is different. There is no set time limit for every person. AA has a wonderful slogan that is so true: "It works if you work it." If you get impatient with yourself and don't take the time to heal, you will only see an illusion of what's right in front of your eyes. Don't you want to see the truth? Even if the truth is painful, wouldn't you rather face it now? Because the truth always comes out eventually.

Emotional healing is different from physical healing. Let's say you have a bruise on your leg. You know when your leg is better because you see the physical signs. The bruise is gone, and you don't have any more pain. But you can't see your heart. So how will you know when you're better emotionally? You'll be in a better frame of mind overall. Your life will be more balanced. You will find yourself making wise decisions about things in general. You'll think more clearly. You won't make a big deal out of everything. You will not be over-the-top angry, or an under-the-foot doormat. You won't cry at the drop of a hat. Your eating and sleeping will balance out. Your emotions will be more stable and centered.

We know of many painful stories from women who think they have to have a man in their lives in order to function, or they don't think life is worth living without being in a relationship. This is not a healthy attitude at all. These women get burned over and over again.

Meet Donna. Donna is a beautiful woman, extremely successful, and was once married to a high-profile man for a number of years. He was attractive and women flocked to him. She'd had it and finally divorced him because of his repeated infidelity. She immediately wanted to get right back into the dating scene. Not long afterward, she met Rich online. He was new in her town, and he wanted to get to know some people. She introduced him to her friends so he could get connected. Donna and Rich seemed to be a great match. His job had transferred him to Atlanta, where she lived, and eventually he was going to move back to his hometown, Seattle, where his children lived. He was upfront with her about this. Although the relationship seemed to be progressing nicely and sparks were flying all over the place, he never mentioned marrying her or having her relocate to his city. They dated for eighteen months, and all was going well. She fell in love with him and consummated the relationship. She was hooked.

One weekend his parents came into town for a visit, and he didn't even bother to introduce them to Donna. She was devastated. She could see that she wasn't high on the totem pole when it came to his priorities. So now she's cooling her jets with him. She's hurt. The thing is, it's not his fault. He laid all his cards on the table to begin with, but she thought she could get him to love her and change his mind about the way this was going to play out. You see, in most cases, the truth is there, right in front of our eyes, and we refuse to see what's really there because we're hopeless romantics.

We are going to candidly share from our hearts some of our own stories and how we finally learned to respect ourselves. We stumbled, fell, and got up a few times before we finally got it.

GIVE YOURSELF TIME

Connie

Since I did not take the time needed to heal after my divorce, it took me twice as long to get to the place where I am now. The Word of God tells us, "Above all else, guard your heart" (Proverbs

4:23). I didn't pay any attention to that because I thought I was a big girl and could handle it. I knew that the divorce produced a ripping apart from the man I had made a covenant with. But I thought I just needed another man to take his place to glue it back together again, and everything would be fine. To me these failed relationships seem like big mistakes. But are they really mistakes? We must make mistakes in order to learn valuable lessons. Even though I'm hard on myself at times, I'm making an effort to change that. I'm trying to be gentler on myself, and I encourage you to be gentle on yourself too.

So there I was, ready to get back in the dating game. I think I had a sign on me that said, "If you're an emotional train wreck and want to mess with someone's head, then I'm your girl." And they came. Why did I attract this type of man? Well, it's because they could sense my woundedness and vulnerability. I was the perfect target. Even though I consider myself to be a fairly intelligent woman, my IQ went right down the drain when it came to men. Either I was too picky, or I wasn't picky enough. I know the kind of man I'd like to have in my life exists. I know lots of them, in fact. There's just one small problem. They're all married . . . to my girlfriends!

So let's go on a man journey, if you will, of the last ten years of my life post-divorce.

Brandon

I've mentioned Brandon several times. In all honesty, as dedicated as he was to me, I could see that he was not a man who could commit. He told me that it took him quite some time to propose to his wife. And she gave him an ultimatum, saying, "We're either getting married, or we're breaking up." So he married her.

Years later they were divorced. Early on, before we got emotionally involved, he shared with me that he wanted children. Because I was much older than he was, I already had grown children. I knew from the get-go that we were at different stages of life, and it just wasn't right. He tried to end it a year after we were dating, but I was such a basket case that I convinced him to come back to the relationship. (Hint: If you have to sell yourself to a guy or convince him to see you or stay with you, you're headed for a crash-and-burn situation.)

I didn't know how I'd function without him. I will go as far as to say that I was addicted to him. Addicted to the relationship. Codependency to the max. I felt like I *needed* him to survive. I think my theme song for several years following our breakup was, "How am I supposed to live without you?" This neediness is a form of idolatry, or some refer to it as codependency. God has shown me that He will not tolerate being second place in my life to anyone or anything. He has also shown me that a healthy person doesn't *need* anyone to make it in this life. Yes, we all have needs—food, shelter, income, social interaction, and so on. We need doctors, lawyers, and certain groups of people to help us live well. But the only one we really need is the One who created us. We are completely whole when we realize that all we need is Him. It's certainly fine to love another person and want someone to share your life with, but when you need him to survive, you're in trouble. As author Melody Beattie eloquently stated in her book *The Language of Letting Go,* "When we've learned to stand on our own two feet, then we're ready to stand next to someone else."[1]

After years of dating, Brandon and I started talking about getting married (actually, I was the one doing most of the talking) and decided we would get engaged sometime the following spring. But still, in the back of my mind I didn't feel like Brandon's heart was in it 100 percent. He seemed tentative about the engagement but was going through the motions. As spring drew closer, we began looking at houses and found one we loved. We were about to sign a contract on a house together and get engaged all in the same weekend. A few days before it was to come down, Brandon was supposed to stop by after a meeting at work. He was late, and it wasn't like him not to call. So I phoned him asking him where he was. He asked me if I had gotten the letter he left in my mailbox earlier that day. I got the sickest feeling in the pit of my stomach. Years invested in this relationship and all I got was a letter in my mailbox breaking it off. This time for good.

I was wrecked for a long time, and the breakup threw me back into counseling. I was grieving the loss of my husband because I didn't take enough time to grieve over my marriage ending. I was grieving the breakup with Brandon. And I was grieving the fact that I had to leave the church I had attended because Brandon went there as well, and it was too painful to see him every week. I tried so hard to be a big girl and go. But every Sunday it was like picking off a scab and letting it bleed over and over again. I had to make the break. My wise counselor said one sentence that changed my life: "It's amazing how the God of the universe pales in comparison to Brandon." It hit me so profoundly. Then I grieved at the way I treated my Lord by putting my relationship with Brandon before Him. Live and learn, right? Not quite.

James

I wish I could say I learned my lesson about waiting to heal before dating again. But it wasn't long before I got right into another relationship with James, about whom I spoke in detail in the chapter on forgiveness. He also was much younger than I. I wasn't looking for younger guys. It's just the way it happened. I was introduced to him through a dear friend at a party only four months after my breakup with Brandon. And of course I jumped right in so that James could be my mand-aid for my broken heart. I tried to convince myself I was over Brandon and ready to start dating again. Do you see a cycle here?

The huge problem in this relationship was that James was going through a divorce. I advise you never to date or even casually see a man who hasn't been single for a couple of years. If he's not divorced, even if he has been separated for some time, he's still married. And if he's still married, then he hasn't gone through his healing, and he's thinking like a teenager. I would also advise against dating a man who's just gotten out of a serious dating relationship. I got burned on that one too. And I will visit that relationship with you later on in this chapter.

I fell hook, line, and sinker for James because of a few things. First, he told me everything I ever wanted to hear and made me feel beautiful. Second, his voice was like "buttuh." I'm a sucker for a guy with a great voice. Third, he had a keen sense of humor and made me laugh. Fourth, he had an appreciation for good music. And last, but certainly not least, he pulled out all the God cards. If he knows Scripture and knows how to pray, I'm captivated.

Take note of the guys you fall for. The men you are attracted to will have a lot of the same qualities. And take note of the type of guys who are attracted to you. Just remember that if the guy is the real deal, he'll put his money where his mouth is. Actions speak much louder than words. You don't need some guy who builds sand castles. Just watch the way he lives his life, and see if his actions match his words. Talk is cheap. It's the *doing* on a consistent basis that proves he's the real deal. Is he consistently dependable? Is he controlling or possessive? How does he interact with his family? Is he on good terms with his parents, siblings, and his children? If not, these are red flags, and you should take note of them. What are red flags for you? Write them down, and if the guy has a red flag, then end it. Of course, you're not going to find a perfect person. Perfect human beings don't exist. But there are things you can live with and things you can't. What are those things for you?

Well, James ended our relationship pretty quickly. That left me thinking that I wasn't good enough again. I never quite made the grade. I fell short. There must have been something majorly wrong with me. And there was. I was a desperate, hurting, broken woman looking for love. And I got it, but it wasn't the right kind of love, and it never lasted. I sobbed for a long time.

David

But not that long, because my friend Annie knew someone she wanted to introduce me to. He was in full-time ministry and had just gone through his second divorce (yellow light—proceed with caution). Annie and her hubby, Jack, knew David for a long time, and they told me what a quality man he was. David was handsome, and women turned their heads when he walked by. He lived in Oklahoma City, so we met on the telephone and had wonderful phone conversations almost every night for a month before we met.

He flew in with flowers, and we double-dated with Annie and Jack. It was major chemistry from the get-go. He was staying in town for the weekend, and we spent every minute we could together. It truly was a romantic weekend with picnics in the park. A candlelit dinner at my place. Praying together. Talking about the Bible. Snuggling on the couch and watching a movie together. Church on Sunday followed by lunch with our friends. I hated to see him leave. It was a magical three days. I brought him to the airport, and when he kissed me good-bye, it was like he was leaving for a year. Then he said, "I'm not going to call you for about a week because I want to process what happened between us this weekend. And I need time to sort through this." Sorry, but I thought that was weird. It didn't seem right after the incredible weekend we just spent together. I told him I thought that it was odd but to go ahead and do what he needed to do. A week later he called and said he missed me. He loved having me in church by his side, and he wanted to continue to talk and date. I was thrilled.

Well, three weeks had gone by, and I hadn't heard a thing from him. So I sent him an e-mail telling him that I was confused because he hadn't been in touch at all. (Hint: If he's not contacting you, he's just not that into you!) So he wrote me a brief e-mail telling me that he had "paralysis of analysis" and decided to put the "love bug" on hold for a while. I replied by telling him to throw the love bug in park with the emergency brake on until he figured out what in the world he was doing. He wrote back asking me why I was so bitter.

The fact of the matter was that David was recently divorced for the second time and really did need to put the love bug in park before he started communicating with me. Annie and Jack were embarrassed and shocked at his behavior, probably more so because he was in ministry. I guess we expect more from them. But at the end of the day, a man is a man.

Alan

A few months later I was at a Sunday school gathering, and I met Alan. He was alone, and he walked right up and introduced himself. Alan was handsome and had just started going to my church. He wanted to get to know some people. So I introduced him to several friends, and I told him the next time he was in church to look for me. And the next Sunday, there he was. We sat together and then went out to lunch. He told me about his work and his family and that he'd been divorced for ten years. Then he told me that his girlfriend had recently broken up with him because they'd been dating for a few years, and she was ready to get married but he wouldn't commit. *Ding, ding, ding! Don't date him, Connie,* said the little voice in my head. But nooo. His blue eyes made me melt. So I gave in and started dating him. Things went well for a few months.

After about three months of dating him, one Saturday he asked me to go shopping with him to pick out a new wardrobe. Well, I'm a fashionista, so I liked the idea of doing that. We had a lot of fun as he tried on things and modeled for me. He laid down a lot of cash that day. The next evening we went to a Christmas party, so I got dolled up and was proud to be going to the party with Alan. On the way home that night, he told me that his ex-girlfriend called him and wanted to see him. He said he was going over for a visit the next evening. Can you see it coming? They got back together, and he married her a few months later. So basically I went out and picked out an entire wardrobe for Alan to impress the woman he still loved. He was just trying to block her out of his mind by dating me.

That episode sent me into a seven- or eight-month sabbatical from men.

Paul

It wasn't long before I got antsy and got on one of those Christian dating websites. I began communicating with a wonderful man. His name was Paul, and he was from up north, close to my birth city, Chicago. Paul was Italian and good looking. And he was meticulous. He dressed like he just walked out of *GQ*, and I loved that about him. He had an incredible sense of style. He had been divorced for five years and had been in one serious relationship since then that had ended two years earlier. He was ready to start dating again. He was responsible. He had longevity in his job. He was a great family man. His children loved him, and he was very close with his parents and his siblings.

We talked on the phone every night and would see each other once a month. Either he'd come to see me, or I'd go up for a visit. I met his family. They seemed like wonderful people. Paul had a beautiful, well-kept home. He loved the Lord. He was a quality man. He was considering relocating to where I lived, and that got me thinking. There was a problem, and it was a big one. I didn't love him. As wonderful as he was, the chemistry just wasn't there. I'm the type of person who knows after two or three dates whether there's chemistry or not. For others it takes longer. But I thought maybe this time it would be different, so I dated him for nine months hoping that the chemistry would suddenly appear. I begged God to help me love him in a romantic sense because he was a good man. After all those failed relationships, I'd finally found a solid man who had all the ingredients to make a great husband, and I couldn't love him. *What was wrong with me?* I wondered. When all the ingredients are there minus the chemistry, all you have is a friendship. It broke my heart to end it with such a great guy, but I couldn't string Paul along any further. I asked myself over and over why I couldn't love the man who had it all together. Why did I love the ones who had major flaws and hurt me?

This is what you have to look at when you go through your counseling. You must look at yourself instead of always looking at the other person. You can only change you, your choices, your outlook, your behavior. Hold up the mirror and look. When you do, you will see someone beautiful who just has some flaws from living life. No one gets by unscathed. No one.

Rick

Now I will tell you about the straw that broke the camel's back for me. You think I would've learned my lesson by now. But no!

A dear friend of mine, Madeline, was dating Roger. One night at dinner Madeline met Roger's friend, Rick. Rick was charming and had been divorced for three years. Madeline liked him instantly. Toward the end of the evening, he asked her if she had any friends she might introduce him to. Madeline has a lot of single women friends, but she thought Rick and I had so much in common. She consulted me about it, and since he lived in another state, I agreed to set up a time when we could talk on the phone. The first time we spoke, he talked nonstop. I could hardly get a word in edgewise, and it turned me off. The next day I told Madeline about his motor mouth and how it turned me off. So she gently said something to him about it. He called me back the next day, and we had a fantastic conversation. We both had each other laughing, and I could tell he was smart, engaging, and had a sense of humor to beat the band.

Soon after, I noticed that he was calling around ten times a day, and I thought that was strange. *Ding! Ding! Ding!* I told him to back off because he was smothering me. He honored my wishes by calling me less often, and when we did talk we had incredible conversations. Rick loved all the same things I did. He was an actor. He loved to read. He had many degrees. He was intelligent. He was also in full-time ministry. He knew the Bible inside and out. He could quote Scripture on a dime and pray his socks off. He had all the components of the type of guy I'm attracted to. (Do you see the pattern?)

His voice was smooth, and I began really looking forward to our phone conversations. I shared with him about my previous heartbreaks and how I'd been through the wringer and just couldn't go through that anymore. He constantly assured me by saying, "I'm a man of integrity. I'm not a flake." If he said that once, he said it a thousand times. I don't want to bore you with *dinging* again, but I really think he was trying to convince himself. Still, I bought it lock, stock, and barrel.

After talking to him on the phone for six weeks every day, I was smitten. We finally agreed to meet, and it was instant head-over-heels chemistry. The relationship progressed quickly after that. He came to visit me and met my family. I went to visit him and met his family. I met his friends. I went to his church and met the pastor. And before I could get hold of myself, we were looking at houses and talking about my relocating to his city and getting married. He talked to me about how we were the perfect couple. We'd do speaking engagements together, write books together, do seminars and marriage workshops. We would truly be helpmates to each other to accomplish God's purpose in our lives. It all sounded so right to me. I couldn't have ordered a guy more suited for me than Rick.

Now, I've told you everything I was attracted to about Rick.

However, Rick had some things about him that were very undesirable. Things that I considered red flags and that I chose to sweep under the rug. Looking back, I'm shocked that I was willing to overlook them. I knew better. And if a friend of mine had been seeing him I would've told her to run like a rabbit, or at least have her head examined. But I couldn't see it in my own life. This is how badly I didn't want to be alone. Thankfully, God saved me from a huge disaster.

About four months after we met, Rick planned a one-week trip for me to come to his city, and he put me up in the most amazing hotel in town. It truly was a magical week. What I didn't know was that he had consulted his pastor earlier about proposing to me, and the pastor gave him his blessing. So one beautiful, summer night, after a romantic dinner, he took me for a walk, got down on one knee, and proposed to me. I said, "Let me think about it . . . Yes!" The next day he put me on the platform at his church and introduced me to the congregation as the woman beyond his dreams—his fiancée, Connie. It was like a fairy tale. And a fairy tale it was, because soon after Prince Charming turned into a frog.

After I accepted his marriage proposal, on the long drive home I began to have panic attacks. Something in my spirit wasn't setting right with this, and I knew it. This surely was the Holy Spirit giving me a warning sign. I wanted to break it off immediately because it was going way too fast, but I couldn't do it. Friends and family wanted to be happy for me but encouraged me to slow things down and get to know him better. But he coerced me to put my house on the market and make plans to move to his city, and reluctantly, I did. Thank God my house didn't sell. Saved by God . . . again!

A month after our engagement, I received an e-mail from Rick asking me to invest a large sum of money in a business deal he was working on. I told him I wouldn't do that, but after we were married, I would work with him and help him save up what he would need to make his dream a reality. From there, things started going downhill. The next morning I woke up to a sobering e-mail about how he couldn't do life with someone who didn't share his dream and wouldn't support him. *Ding! Ding! Ding! Bail, Connie, bail!* said the voice in my head. But did I do it? No! I called him and tried to convince him what a beautiful thing we had going and tried to talk him into looking at it my way. He said I was trying to manipulate him.

Communication was getting less frequent between us. I saw a different side of him. I was supposed to be visiting him the next week so we could put a deposit on a house with *my* money because he was not in a financial position to do so. But the day before I was to leave, he called and simply said, "I have to take this relationship off the table." He went from being as high as a kite to a big downer within six months. I want you to know that I thank God from the bottom of my heart that Rick did for us what I could not do. He broke it off. Thank You, Jesus! I haven't heard from him since.

It was then that I realized the total lack of respect I had for myself in this situation and the others as well. I was willing to buy a home with my money and tie the knot with a man who asked me for more money to invest in his business deal and had more red flags than the United Nations. I was willing to settle. I wasn't brave enough to end it. That's how much I disrespected myself. It took this relationship to finally make me see the light.

Since then, I've taken a hiatus from dating. In this time, I've learned that relationships with men are lessons. They're opportunities to get it right. And unless we heal, most of us are stuck at fourteen to sixteen years of age. Without healing, all we see are illusions, and we will keep coming up with the counterfeit guy. I decided I needed to take some time to figure out why I kept repeating the same unhealthy patterns over and over again.

Merriam-Webster defines the word *respect* as "holding someone in high or special regard."[2] I hadn't been doing that. And it was high time I did.

A dear friend of mine gave me one of the most incredible books I've ever read on Valentine's Day 2008. And this book showed me a beautiful picture of what true love looks like. It's called *Redeeming Love,* by Francine Rivers.[3] It is a fictional story about a love between a man and a woman that coincides with the book of Hosea in the Old Testament. It's about Michael Hosea's love for a prostitute named Angel and how he pursues her in spite of all her imperfections. How he loves her unconditionally. I wept at the beauty of this love story. Every woman in the world wants to be loved that way. And we are—by our Lord and Savior, Jesus. Yet we put ourselves in a category that makes us feel like we are not good enough and must settle for Ishmael when God wants to give us Isaac. My friend signed the inside cover of the book, and it said, "This, my friend, is God's best." And it is. There's nothing better than the love of our Redeemer. And it's ours. This does not mean that we can't desire an earthly husband to share our lives with. And it's more than okay to want that, pray for that, and believe that for our lives. But unless the *right* one comes along, isn't it best to wait?

To wrap this up, I want to let you know how invaluable all my sweet girlfriends are. They've stood by me through my dating relationships and watched my heart break over and over again.

They've challenged me and helped me want to become a better woman. That's what good friends do. They hold you accountable and want to see you grow and become whole and healthy. They want to see you respect yourself enough to hold on to your values and not back down.

WATCH FOR THE RED FLAGS

Michelle

Respect yourself. That is something I didn't learn to do as a young person and thus didn't do as an adult woman after my divorce. Like Connie, I, too, made lots of mistakes trying to figure it all out. There is a song by Willie Nelson, "Somebody Pick Up My Pieces," that was definitely my theme song for a couple of years. The lyrics are telling for those who have encountered divorce: "Somebody pick up my pieces. I'm scattered everywhere."

The truth is, no one can pick up your pieces except God Himself. This is where we end up not respecting ourselves and compromising our values. We are hoping, longing, and desiring someone to come along and lift us up, but God is the lifter of our heads. Are you hoping a man will pick you up and take away the pain? It's amazing how quickly all our values go out the window if we are searching for someone to medicate our pain.

Don't do it. Here are some trappings to look for as you step out into this new world of being single. Connie and I want you to be aware of scenarios we were totally unaware of. I personally was very naive to the ways of people and their ability to take advantage of the weak. It's the way life works. If you are vulnerable and naive, and someone who does not have a good heart wants something from you, he will find a way to take it. This is why it's important to have boundaries and a plan in place and be aware of the trappings.

There are married men who look for weak-willed women. They are called predators, and they seek out women who are vulnerable and in a place of instability. For example, my friend Cindy found herself in a horrible situation. She has always held high standards and values, but after her divorce, she was an emotional wreck, and her mind and heart were not stable, so it was easy for someone to come in and deceive her.

Gary was someone she really respected and cared for as a friend. He asked to meet with her on the guise he needed some advice on his impending divorce. She was just coming out of an abusive relationship and had not been divorced long herself, so she was not in any position to be giving advice; but she felt safe with him, and they were friends so she thought nothing of it. They met a few times, and she would listen to his pain and give him advice until one night he followed her home from work. She looked in her rearview mirror, and there he was. Even then she thought it only a coincidence. He called and asked if she was in front of him, and she of course replied yes. He then asked if she wanted to meet him for a drink.

She had never crossed that line with him, but they were beginning to feel more comfortable, so she agreed. She didn't fall that night, but it was the beginning of a two-week relationship that could have eventually destroyed her had she not caught on to his lies. She found out he was not getting a divorce and that she was not the first woman he had lied to. This was a pattern for him—only this time it backfired.

She felt so horrible she called someone she knew who would

hold her accountable in the situation and told her the story. She was really struggling to let him go because he was telling her all the things she needed to hear. Things like, "I want to take care of you and your children for the rest of your lives," "I've never loved anyone like you," "You are the most beautiful woman in the world." It was hard for her to resist him so she exposed the relationship to a friend who in turn stepped in and intervened.

Cindy didn't have the strength to let him go. She needed the guidance of a friend to help her make the decision. She immediately cut all ties to him, and even then he called her after he'd been drinking and left a message on her voice mail that he needed her. She never responded. Two years later he went through a divorce and called her to see if there was a chance they could reconnect. By this time Cindy had emotionally done the hard work and was much healthier and, looking back, realized his motives at the time. She not only had no interest in hearing from him, but she also realized how easily she could have been deceived and gone down a path that would have only done further damage to her soul. In the long run, she respected herself and did not allow herself to be used.

Pam, on the other hand, was not as wise. She spent a year dating a high-profile, married man who told her all the same things and said he was divorcing and leaving his wife. When she finally pushed him to see if he was telling the truth, he called and told her he could not see her anymore because he had decided to stay with his family. In both cases I was there for these women. My heart went out to Cindy and Pam, and I never once told Pam I told you so. She knew her mistakes without me even telling her, and after he broke ties with her, she immediately repented and began to get her life in order to heal.

Some married men look for single women to seduce. Beware of these men. They know what you need, what you want to hear, and that you don't have the willpower to resist. Remember to look for character, not charm. Charming men say all the right things, but the character and heart of a person is what is important.

Be careful not only of married men but also of men with emotional baggage. I remember having a conversation with Stephen Arterburn, a well-known author who deals with men's issues. I said to him, "Steve, I am looking for someone void of issues, who can love me just as I am and doesn't have a bunch of baggage." He said something very profound: "Michelle, there is no one without baggage. What you need to decide is what baggage you are willing to live with, and see if he is willing to face and deal with the issues." So very true. If you are looking for Mr. Perfect, the bad news is he doesn't exist—but the good news is you are less-than-perfect yourself.

So what do we do about baggage and issues? Here are some signs to look for when it comes to respecting yourself and yet having mercy so you can actually meet someone and possibly one day marry.

1. Don't make excuses for the person. It's so easy to rationalize away the red flags. Be honest about who the person is.
2. Don't look at the person's potential for changing or becoming what you want him to be. Most people don't change. Instead, look at his desire to grow. Does he want to become better? Is he willing to go to counseling with you to work through his issues?
3. Decide what you can live with and what you cannot. For example, can you live with a smoker? Can you live with

someone who has struggled with pornography? Don't compromise your "live with" and "live without" list.

4. Make a list of how you can know he is "just not that into you."

Back in my dating days, I had a casual relationship with Tom, whom I met and had coffee with for about six months at Starbucks. We kept it totally friendship but talked about marriage and other things related to being together. I really cared for him, but he seemed so distant. I thought he was just trying to be cautious and respectful. He was a speaker, and I'd go hear him speak now and then. My daughter came with me once, and after the event he came up to me to say hello, and his body language appeared distant.

Afterward, Madison said to me, "Mom, why are you wasting your time with this guy? He is not into you at all." Out of the mouth of babes. Sometimes it takes someone else to tell us when someone is not respecting us and giving us the attention and care we deserve. I spent six months with the guy, and nothing had changed. What other evidence did I need?

After the guy I went with who was abusive and a sex addict, I was so cautious. I ran every guy by people I respected. I felt my judgment and discernment could be easily skewed by other emotions such as being lonely. I actually ended relationships based on other people's observations. Remember, it was always people I trusted, and I even ended one on my kid's observation. When you realize your own judgment can't be counted on alone, it's important to call in the troops. Thank God for those people in my life.

Respecting yourself is also about knowing your value. It's

important to really know who you are in Christ. Here are a few things you should ask yourself:

Do I feel

- Anxious?
- Worthless?
- Incompetent?
- Insignificant?
- Hopeless?
- Unacceptable?
- Helpless?
- Unloved?
- Used?
- Depressed?
- Uncertain about myself and God?

Or do I feel

- Confident?
- Competent?
- Significant?
- Successful?
- Secure?
- Worthy?
- Loved?

Do I reject truth, renounce truth, rebuke truth, and rebel against truth?

Or do I embrace truth, speak truth, will truth, act in truth, become truth, and grow as a result of truth?

Ask yourself these questions, and if you lean more toward the negative responses, I would say you don't value yourself and you see yourself as a victim. If you lean toward the positive answers, I would say you do value yourself and therefore can respect yourself.

Here are some promises in Scripture to help you know your value:

- I am God's child (John 1:12).
- I am free from condemnation (Romans 8:1–2).
- I am not afraid (2 Timothy 1:7).
- I am born of God, and the evil one cannot touch me (1 John 5:18).
- I can do all things through Christ (Philippians 4:13).

Work up your spiritual muscles, and begin to build yourself from the ground up. Find someone who is a great friend, and ask her to help build you up weekly. Someone who pours the Word into you is water to your thirsty soul.

In order to respect yourself, you have to know your value—and in order to know your value, you have to see yourself through God's filter. He sees us through the blood of the Lamb, spotless and blameless. Our righteousness alone is not able to cover our sin. It took Christ dying on the cross, sacrificing His life so that we might be free. It's a free gift of love. When we choose Christ, we are saying, *I am forgiven because of the sacrifice He made. Because I am forgiven, I can forgive others and love unconditionally.* When our perspective is filtered through the lens of God's Word, we are able to walk in freedom and feel secure with who we are in Christ. Freedom is a beautiful thing, and wholeness in Christ is even more beautiful than ever.

YOU and Respect Thoughts

We want to revisit the subject of professional, faith-based counseling. So many of the decisions we make reflect what we grew up with, what we learned when we were young girls. We know how important it is to unpack all that baggage, sort through it, and discard what needs to be discarded. It is healing to revamp what needs a little overhauling and keep the good stuff. We are not suggesting that you stay in counseling for the rest of your life. Who could afford that? But you may find that you need to go back to your counselor for a tune-up from time to time or to visit new situations in your life that are so complicated you need a little help. That's okay. That's what counselors are there for. And you're not going to gel with all counselors. You may have to go through a few before you find a good fit. If you don't have counseling sessions on your insurance plan, there are professionals who will work with you on a sliding scale based on your income level. And there are some free counseling centers as well.

We hope that in sharing our own stories you have gleaned something you could apply to your own life. Maybe you see yourself in our stories. You know, we're not all that different from one another. As you grow to be emotionally healthy, you will begin to realize your value in Christ, to respect yourself as a true woman of God—a woman of royal destiny.

YOU and Respect Actions

- Don't settle . . . *period.*
- Don't date a man who just got out of a serious

relationship or is not completely, legally divorced and has been for at least a year.

- When you see a red flag, end it now. Remember, red flags are nonnegotiable.
- Look at the way he lives his life. Look at what he does, not at what he says. Talk is cheap.
- Have a good accountability person in your life. Run potential mates by your good friends and get their take on them.
- If something smells fishy, it is. If something doesn't add up, it doesn't. Trust the Holy Spirit and the good conscience God blessed you with to discern what is good and right and what isn't.

YOU and Respect Prayer

Lord Jesus, Your Word tells me that my Maker is my husband . . . the Lord of hosts is His name. I know that only You can truly fill the longing in my soul. But Your Word also tells me that it is not good for man to be alone, for two are better than one. When I am ready, and if it's Your will, Lord, bring me a man who is an earthly representation of Your love. Help us cross paths at the right time. Bring me a man who models his life according to the Word of God.

Do a work in my life, Lord, helping me be a whole and healthy woman. Heal my heart and help me guard it at all times. Teach me to love and respect myself the way You do. Give me wisdom and discernment in all my relationships. When and if the right man comes along, help me love and respect him in a healthy way, not with a spirit of neediness or idolatry but with a love between a man and woman as You intended it to be. Help me keep You first in all things, believing that everything else will fall into place according to Your perfect plan. Praying these things in the precious name of my Lord and Savior, Jesus, amen.

eight
THE ULTIMATE YOU PLAN

Time is a precious commodity, and as we all know it flies by at the speed of lightning. So *now* is the time to craft a plan for your life. We know that God ordains all our steps (Psalm 37:23). But He gives you the beautiful gift of freedom to choose what you want to do with your life. You have options. What a wonderful gift. The Ultimate YOU Plan involves cleaning your internal house. It's time to get rid of the emotional clutter that is weighing you down and burdening your soul. In fact, we suggest physically making the motion of brushing all the negativity off of your body with your hands and then shaking your hands free of all the toxic stuff that comes with internalizing junk. It's time to begin filling yourself up with all things good and positive. And yes, it is possible to do that in the midst of turbulence.

We told you in earlier chapters that the only way you can change what is, is by accepting where you are and who you are. Only after this realization are you free to be who you want to be and go where you want to go. We also mentioned the importance of forgiveness. In order to move on in any way, you will have to come to a place of forgiving those who have wronged you, and you will have to forgive yourself. This is what God says we must do according to His Word. No option on this one. The act of forgiveness releases us and frees us to move on and do great things.

Diana Scharf Hunt once said, "Goals are dreams with deadlines." Oh, how true this is. You can dream your whole life, but without an action plan and the goals laid out to get there, you may end this life floating away on your dreams instead of your successes. The last thing we want you to feel is more stress. Stress is a huge part of divorce, especially if you have kids. Writing down your goals and creating the Ultimate YOU Plan is not meant to stress you out; it's meant to relieve stress in your life. The more you have a plan, the less you have to worry about what the next step is.

Vision is important to laying out your goals, and every vision begins with a basic mission statement. So let's write a mission statement for your life. Don't worry, you can change it any time. Just start right now with what you feel is a good mission for your life.

Really think this one through. You are on a mission. And believe us, it's not mission impossible. Because with God *all* things are possible (Matthew 19:26). What do you stand for? What makes your heart sing? What ignites your passion? What is your purpose? What are your intentions? What inspires you or motivates you? What are the desires of your heart? What are your goals? Just start writing them down. Create an outline, and then begin to craft your mission statement as concisely as possible. It should not be too long. Just a paragraph. You might want to focus on two to three areas, such as your finances, health, or relationship with God.

Then come up with a strategy on how you're going to achieve the things you've written about. Also come up with time frames that are reasonable so you can see the progress you've made. Consistency and discipline are the main keys to getting the job done. Pray over your mission statement and give it to God. We suggest doing a mission statement every year. You don't have to drastically change it. Maybe just a little tweaking. Your birthday is a good time to do it. You will see that your dreams, plans, goals, and visions will change from time to time as your life evolves in different ways.

We will begin to break the Ultimate YOU Plan into categories, many of which have been covered in this book. If you don't feel that you need to work on that area, then let it go. You may want to create new categories that we don't mention. Tailor-make your plan to suit you.

YOU AND CAREER

"I hate my job," you say. Or "It's just a job." Or "I can't quit because I make a great salary and I have good benefits." Since you spend so much time in the workplace, shouldn't you be doing something you enjoy? Something that is suited to your gifts and talents? If you need extra classes to achieve that goal but can't go to school full-time, you can probably afford to take one class at a time. Eventually, you'll get there. Just keep chipping away. Maybe you want to start your own business. Or maybe you have started your own business but you're not generating enough revenue yet to do it full-time. Perhaps you need a part-time job to fill in the financial gap until your business takes off. We highly recommend career counselor Dan Miller's books *48 Days to the Work You Love* and *No More Mondays*. We also recommend Dave Ramsey's book *Entrée Leadership*. These are great reads on helping you craft a career that you will enjoy.

A young single mother we know wants to be a special education teacher. She has a rough, demanding life caring for two little ones on her own. But she works as an aide at a school and helps mentally challenged children. She also takes babysitting jobs on the weekends when she can, caring for children with special needs. When her children's dad has the kids, she takes one class at a time toward fulfilling her goal. She hopes to be done with her classes so that when her second child is in school full-time, she will have graduated and be gainfully employed as a special ed teacher.

Put the plan in motion. You know the story of the tortoise and the hare. Just keep going in the right direction and don't slack off. You know how it ends. The tortoise always wins.

YOU AND FINANCES

With the economy as it is right now, everybody is feeling it in the pocketbook. If you are a lousy money manager, now is the time to learn how to be a better one. It doesn't matter how broke you are. We suggest that every time you get a paycheck, you bank something. It could be five dollars. Don't tell us you can't save at least five dollars. That's what you pay for a venti latte at Starbucks. You just need to be sick and tired of being broke and be determined to change your financial future. Building a savings plan is important, because something will always come up where you need money for emergencies.

We have a friend who saves all year in a Christmas fund to buy presents for her family and friends. When that time of the year rolls around, she has a certain amount of money set aside. She budgets for each gift and it's all paid for. Then she doesn't have Visa chasing her after the holidays. Create a monthly budget, and incorporate savings and giving into your budget.

Paying off debt is very liberating. Start chipping away at it a little at a time. Depending on your financial situation, if you have any debt at all and not a lot of money in the bank, take out a term life insurance policy that is substantial enough to pay off your debt and take care of your burial expenses. Generally term life policies are very inexpensive. This is the responsible thing to do for your family members.

We recommend getting a disability income policy in the event you become disabled. Then you will have income coming in. You may be able to get it through your workplace. If you're self-employed like we are, you can shop your own policy. This is extremely important for single people. If you don't have any income coming in but your own, then you can't afford not to have this type of insurance.

If you don't have a will, please do that pronto. This, too, is the responsible thing to do. Don't you want to make your own decisions about what you have and to whom you want it to go? Do you really want a family feud over your things? And if you were unable to make decisions for yourself, wouldn't you want to designate someone to make decisions on your behalf? All of this is handled in your will.

YOU AND HEALTH

Honestly, one of the best gifts you can have in the land of the living is good health. If you don't have that, it's hard to get the other things in place. We're not just talking physical health. We're talking about the whole YOU.

Your Physical YOU

Take care of the temple God gave you. We know it's easy to gain weight during a divorce or lose too much weight. It's time to get back on track. You are not doing yourself any favors medicating on food or starving yourself. If your eating is out of control, you may need a fitness coach. If you can't afford a coach or gym membership, a good pair of walking shoes will get you moving. And if you are not eating and are leaning toward mental breakdown in this area, please see someone who can help you get back on track.

Sometimes when our lives feel out of control, we suddenly look for ways to control; yet in our control over food, we find we are enslaved to it. What masters us controls us. Don't allow food, alcohol, or drugs to control and enslave your life. Instead, eat healthy foods, get on track with eating enough calories instead of too few, and focus less on weight and more on being healthy. Don't let food, alcohol, or drugs be an addiction that feeds your emotional bankruptcy. It will only take you down deeper into feeling less valued and more insecure.

Your Emotional YOU

It takes a great deal of determination to pursue your emotional health. It's tedious, even gut-wrenching at times, but it is what will bring you to the place of emotional wholeness.

Your emotional health can affect your physical health if you do not address it. Find someone safe, whether it be a counselor, a pastor, or a life coach. Spend time with them, opening up your life and allowing them to give you feedback as to how you can heal. For some, the emotional wound goes way back. For others, it's mostly the pain from the divorce. Press through and fight for it with everything in you. Your freedom is worth it.

Your Mental YOU

Mental health is essential to walking out the new YOU plan. It's not easy to detect after a divorce exactly when you feel you are mentally healthy and ready to begin stepping into new territory. Initially, it takes every bit of mental and emotional strength just to make it through a day. We understand this. If you are still here, then you are not quite ready for the Ultimate YOU Plan, but don't lose hope. It won't be long before you are ready to begin to walk out your new life and will even begin to have moments of enjoying it. If you feel you are mentally struggling, please know it is not abnormal, and you are not losing your mind. You have experienced one of the most traumatic experiences you will ever encounter, so don't be afraid to spend some time doing whatever it takes to become mentally healthy again. Addressing the spiritual and the emotional will help in this area too.

Your Spiritual YOU

This area is most important. It's so easy during this time to become isolated from what you need most, from what will feed your thirsty soul. When you feel abandoned, deserted, and depressed, it's easy to fall away from your lifeline for a time, but don't. This is the one thing the enemy will try to steal from you. If he can keep you bitter, if he can keep you depressed and discouraged or angry with God, he will keep you from walking out the Ultimate YOU Plan. Not only that, he will keep you from becoming healthy and whole again. You need more than ever before to walk closely with the Lord. It's God's strength that needs to fill you. It's His wisdom you will need to guide you, and it's His Spirit, the Holy Spirit, who will help you not to walk in the flesh and fail again and again.

Don't throw away the one thing that will save you. If you can't sit in church—and many women just can't go to church alone when they are first divorced—then find a small church group to be a part of. There are singles' programs at churches or weekday programs that are less intimidating. You need connection and relationships. Don't allow the enemy to get you isolated. When we are left to our own devices, our thinking can become stinking thinking. Remember iron sharpens iron. We understand it's hard to get back into the social scene. Find those who have gone through similar circumstances so you can feel safe as you share.

A Healthy YOU

Don't take your health on any level for granted. Take care of the temple God gave you. Be kind to it. Eat right. Exercise regularly. Sleep seven to eight hours per night. Don't slack off on this stuff. It's important. We know it's hard to "be good" all the time. On this one, the 80/20 rule is reasonable. The 85/15 rule is even better. Eighty percent of the time be on mark, but then give yourself grace for that 20 percent of life that causes you to have too many desserts (Christmas), miss a workout, or not sleep well. Believe us, we're preaching to the choir on this one.

Make sure you get your yearly physicals. Research things you put in your body before taking them. Ask your doctor questions. You know your body. If something doesn't seem right, get it checked out. And please, don't Google health issues. It'll raise your level of anxiety and make you think the worst possible thing is going on.

We're convinced that there are two things that can contribute to getting sick. The first is stress. There is article after article to back up that statement. The best solution is to remove yourself from stressful situations as much as possible, but sometimes we can't do that. So learn tools to help you manage stress and keep it at bay. The second is the condition of your heart. We're not talking about the physical condition of your heart, but the emotional and spiritual condition of it. The Word of God tells us: "Above all else, guard your heart, for everything you do flows from it" (Proverbs 4:23). Every issue—relationships, health, work—is affected by the condition of your heart.

Here is another key verse to monitor the condition of your heart. The Word of God tells us, "Get rid of all bitterness, rage and anger, brawling and slander, along with every form of malice. Be kind and compassionate to one another, forgiving each other, just as in Christ God forgave you" (Ephesians 4:31–32). My friend, if you are hanging on to these things, you will eventually make yourself physically ill. Let it go and pursue your freedom. Rid yourself of toxic behavior and relationships.

If you're in need of counseling to get you through a rough time, then take the time to do that to restore your mental and emotional health. We don't suggest that you stay in counseling forever. In fact, we believe it's harmful to keep rehashing the same painful stuff over and over again. Unpack your baggage once and empty it out, deal with it, and move on as best you can.

There is a huge payoff for taking care of your health. As they say, it's not quantity but quality. We all want to live as long as possible. Taking care of your overall health will improve your quality of life.

YOU AND KIDS

It doesn't matter how old your children are; if you have kids, you're still concerned about them no matter what their ages are.

Remember that you are the parent. Exercise that right by being consistent in your love and discipline. Live a life of doing more than saying. Your kids are watching you, and you will set the example by what you do. They did not want or ask for the divorce, yet the divorce happened to them too.

If you divorced when your kids were young, it's not easy for them to process. Sometimes it will be years before they actually process what happened. This happened to Michelle. Her kids began going to counseling in their late teens when they were able to think through what had happened to them as young children. Be supportive and don't take it personally. You may have already grieved and moved on, but your children may not start the grieving process until much later.

Please don't expect your older children to be your counselors. Don't expect them to understand your hurt and pain regarding the demise of your marriage. Don't expect them to make you feel better by dissing your ex. That is not their job. And please, please, please don't bash their dad. When you do that, you're bashing them. They are a part of their father just like they are a part of you. We have a friend who honestly didn't have many nice things to say about her ex. He was the guy who went out and married the girl a few years older than their oldest daughter, an abuser, and a very self-absorbed person. I am sure it was hard to think of much to say about this man, but our friend looked for things to say, like, "Your daddy has a good voice" or "Your daddy does a great job at helping you with math." Do the best you can to lift him up without being false. They will see through that.

Set boundaries. Make sure you have enough "me" time and enough time with your children. Even if you have to go in your room for twenty minutes to have some peace and quiet while they do an activity in another room, take the time. If your children are too little to do that, perhaps you can work something out with a friend who also has little ones to swap babysitting duties for a couple of hours each week.

Before bringing another significant other into their lives, please realize that this will be a huge transition for them. Don't do it too soon. Make time for the dust to settle, and get used to the new normal of having a split-up family. Even after time has passed, make sure to not introduce them to a dating partner until you really know the relationship is long term. They don't need to be dragged through one relationship after another. Our dear children pay a *huge* price for our broken families. It's not their fault. Make them a priority when choosing another mate.

Holidays are especially hard. You have to designate time for your children to spend with your ex and his family and you and your family. Try to make this as easy as possible for your children. The more tension there is between you and your ex, the worse it is for your children. We both have had to be at events with our former spouses and make it a point to work with them when it comes to the best interest of the kids. Unless your former spouse was abusive or had other issues that would be detrimental to your kids, try hard to put the past behind you and work toward the best interest of your children. Again, why should they have to suffer any more?

Overall, pray, pray, and pray for your babies (big or small). We are convinced that God loves them far more than we do and will honor our prayers for our children.

YOU AND BEING ALONE

In John 15 we read Jesus' words, "Remain [some versions say abide] in Me and I will remain [abide] in you." This is proof from the Word of God that we are not alone. In fact, we are never alone. The Holy Spirit lives in us and through us. We know, you're saying, "I need human contact." Yes, we do. God has created us to be in relationship with one another and not just in a romantic sense.

We know many people who do absolutely fine on their own. And then there are "people persons" who do much better with "bodies" around and having lots of activity in their lives. It's the difference between introverts and extroverts. We know people who are on their own who have very rich, full lives because of the things they're involved in. There are a number of ways to get involved in great relationships and activities that will allow you to meet people with similar interests. You must craft the life you want. Pray over it and give it to God.

There are Meet Up groups. These groups have hiking clubs, dinner clubs, knitting clubs, foreign language clubs, movie outings, etc. You name it, there's a meet up group that will work for you in practically every city. And they're free.

Hopefully, you are part of a church. There are ministries within that church that are suited to your interests and callings. Make yourself available to that ministry. Pouring into other peoples' lives will bless you in more ways than you can imagine. Join a ladies Bible study, a book club, a class, or the choir, Visit hospitals and the homebound, help out in the children's ministry, or join a supper club. Maybe your church has home fellowship groups. Seeing people week after week will help you form friendships that last.

Volunteering in the community is a good way to meet people. Help out at the local food bank, a thrift shop, the rescue mission, or join the neighborhood cleanup committee.

Join a gym or take an exercise class. You'll see the same people and relationships will begin to form. You'll be doing your body, mind, and spirit some good, and making a friend or two at the same time.

Connie remembers when her Dad retired. He went to the local coffee shop at the same time every morning and began to meet other retirees there. They started the day with a little coffee and fellowship. Before long, they were planning outings outside the coffee shop.

If you have children in school, get involved in volunteering at the school: the library, field trips, the school clinic, the bookstore, etc. There are countless ways to get involved and form friendships.

If you can't stand living alone, maybe you are in a position to take in a roommate. This will not only help you out financially, but will give you some companionship. Or maybe you would be the one renting space in someone else's home. There are lots of things to consider before doing this, but this option could be a win-win for both parties involved.

We can't tell you enough how invaluable it is to have good girlfriends in your life. Connie has a core group of women who are rich in quality personality traits. They are strong, confident, loving, supportive women of God who know how to have fun.

They have prayed with her, encouraged her, laughed and cried with her and have been there through thick and thin. These women have challenged her and held her accountable, making her want to be a better woman overall--a woman of integrity who doesn't settle. If you have one friend like this, you are a blessed woman. Cherish that friendship, nurture it, and reciprocate.

Michelle was single for seven years and also learned to connect with a core group of women who became her support. It's essential. Whether you are single or married, you need your girlfriends. We have learned so much from them. Girlfriends love you through the ups and downs of your life. They rejoice when you rejoice and mourn and weep with you.

And when you are ready, be open to the possibility of dating. Have fun with it. Be selective. Ask God to guard your heart and give you wisdom and discernment. If it's in God's best plan for you, He will bring it to pass. Be content where you are. Lay your hearts desires before God, put forth your best effort and let Him orchestrate your life as it should be.

There is a big difference in being lonely and being alone. We want to re-enforce what we said at the beginning of this section. You are never really alone.

YOU AND DATING

We've talked a lot about dating relationships in this book, and here's the bottom line: *don't settle.* Respect and communication are the main components in making any relationship work well. If you are emotionally healthy and he seems like a good guy, date him. Have fun. Learn all you can about him, his children, and his family. Observe the way he lives. *Take it slow.* If the first red flag shows up, end it right away. Don't prolong the breakup. Again, we realize that perfection does not exist. But a red flag is a red flag. Don't compromise on this one. You are not going to change who he is at the core, and marrying you isn't going to change him either.

Or maybe you've been dating someone and things have been going peachy, then suddenly the relationship takes a turn and he's not calling you anymore and not making an effort to see you. Then realize that if he's not calling, he's just not that into you—but God is. We want the best for you, and we'd rather you go solo then end up with Mr. Wrong. We understand that God has wired us to be in relationship. We understand that for many women, it is their hearts' desire to have that special someone. Pray about it. Give it to God and let it go. Put yourself out there and be open to meeting new people. Just be wise and a bit skeptical.

Run him by your good girlfriends. Get their take on him. They can probably see him a lot clearer than you can. Also, if he's controlling and demanding of your time and doesn't want you to see your friends, then that's a red flag. Just because you're dating someone, it doesn't mean you don't need your friends anymore. We see this happen a lot. If a woman isn't dating, she's hanging out with the girls. If she has a man in her life, she doesn't ever have time for her friends. What kind of a friend is that? Any one group of people that consumes all your time makes for an unhealthy, unbalanced lifestyle. We realize that if you are remarried, of course your husband is your first priority.

YOU AND SEX

Oh, the dilemma of this issue. We feel your pain. If you claim to be a Christian woman, you have a relationship with Christ, and you want to live according to the Word, you know what the Bible says about the issue of sex outside of marriage. How far is too far? You know the answer to this one. This is not thus saith Connie Wetzell or Michelle Borquez. This is the Word of God. Don't do it, until you say "I do." End of story.

YOU AND LOVE

Love shows itself in many different ways. Some people we talk to say, "What is love?" It is perfectly explained in 1 Corinthians 13, which tells us what love is and what love isn't. Is it a feeling or is it a choice? It's both. Sometimes the feeling comes first, and then it's a choice. Here is an example of love in the romantic sense.

Two people fall in love. The feelings of love are overwhelming. They decide to marry. Now life happens, and it's not a bed of roses every day, and sometimes the one you've tied the knot with annoys you or does something that hurts your feelings or just wakes up on the wrong side of the bed. But still you choose to love that person regardless. Or at least that's the way it should be.

True love is unconditional, and Jesus sets the example of love in the purest form and highest degree. He loves perfectly, and none of us can understand the depth, width, height, and enormity of that love. As we become more like Him and walk in the Spirit, that type of love evolves within us. Strive to be more like Him.

We wish you abundance in all good things, but most of all *love*. If you choose not to forgive, if you choose to be angry, you are choosing a path other than love. God's love is so great He has forgiven us for our sins. Think about that. Your sin, your past, your future failures, He has already forgiven it all. It's hard to fathom, and yet He also requires the same of us. Leave the revenge, unforgiveness, and anger at the foot of the cross and choose to love so you can live again.

YOU AND GOD

God is the umbrella over all the other things that concern you. He is all you really need. He is your Lover, Shepherd, Counselor, Redeemer, Friend, and Husband. Relationship with Him is what your soul truly longs for. We keep trying to stuff the emptiness, the longing, with men, toys, plastic surgery, status, wealth, new this and new that; though none of them is wrong, they will not fulfill us . . . ever. Putting God first above all else is the key to success in all the other areas of your life.

We encourage you to take some time every day to nurture your relationship with the One who loves you more than you can imagine, the One who created you with a purpose and a plan. Spend time reading His Word, talking with Him, pouring out your heart to Him, sitting in silence and listening to what He has to say. Dig deeper into that relationship. Invest mightily in it. Take time to see His majesty in creation. Take a little bit of time every day thanking Him and praising Him for who He is . . . in good times and in bad. Oh, how He loves that.

Like you need food for the body to operate efficiently, you

need to take the time to feed yourself the Bread of Life to fill you up spiritually. You don't want to go into spiritual deprivation or starvation mode.

A pastor gave a beautiful analogy of faith. He used a chair to sit on. He explained that he trusted the chair, beyond the shadow of a doubt, that it would hold the full weight of his body. So he sat on it without the slightest bit of worry. This, he says, is how we should demonstrate our faith in God—by placing the full weight of our bodies, souls, and minds on believing in the promises of His Word, never doubting for one second that He has our backs. He's going to deliver. He's going to take care of us, no matter what. Does this strike a chord with you? We suddenly are in awe and feel the need to repent of the needless worrying and fear that goes along with being a single person. Don't let fear and worry become an idol. Let's cast all our anxieties on Him because He cares for us like no other. Let's trust that even when we're going through the really hard stuff that He's going to work every situation out for our good (Romans 8:28) and bring us beauty for ashes (Isaiah 61:3). That's what His Word says. Believe it!

There is no greater love than His.

YOU AND BALANCE

We also want to bring up the importance of balance. Make sure you have all the important elements in your life working together. If you're always doing one thing, like working all the time, and you never have any downtime, then you're out of whack. It's best to have a little of this and a little of that. A little work, a little play. Time with friends, time for your children, and a little me time. Time to indulge, time to hold back. Time with God. If we're one-sided, it could cause us to be anxious or depressed. Balance is important.

We understand initially after your divorce balance will be hard. It takes time to get that equilibrium back in check. Just know that should be your goal. You may have to say no to things you used to say yes to when you were married, but you can say yes to new things. *You* things. If you have joint custody and your former spouse has the children, take time for you. Make a plan before he gets there so you can make the most of your "me" time. If you have your children 100 percent of the time, try to work out a plan with family members or trusted friends to watch the children so you can have some "me" time.

Try new things now and then. A new activity, a new class, a new route to work, a new look. New things promote growth.

And the Ultimate YOU Plan is not just about you. It's about others. Reach out to others. Volunteer. Help someone. Get involved in some type of outreach or ministry that is suited to your interests, calling, and time constraints. Remember, it's all about balance. Taking the focus off yourself and putting it onto others works twofold—you will bless them, and in return you will be blessed as well.

YOU AND MISTAKES

One of the last things we want to leave you with is this: You may wonder why some of the things you banked on so heavily didn't work out for you. And you may find it difficult to trust yourself to make good and right choices. We believe that sometimes we need to make mistakes to learn important lessons we may not otherwise learn. If we are making repeated mistakes in our decisions concerning business, friendships, love, and so on, we may need to learn why we continually walk in the same path. What are we missing?

But again, don't be too hard on yourself. Most of us get it eventually. We grow from our mistakes. We begin to see improvements in the paths we're choosing, thus making us feel good about ourselves. It takes time and wisdom, and everybody's time clock is different. God will allow us to go through the same mess over and over until we finally realize the truth. He doesn't like it. But He allows it.

Now that we've given you some ideas on how the Ultimate YOU Plan works, you will want to incorporate categories that are specific to you. Remember, you have choices. You have options. Choose wisely. Always do the next right thing in every situation and live well.

The Ultimate YOU Plan Checklist

- Accept where you are and who you are, then you'll know where you want to go.
- Forgive, forgive, forgive.
- Create your mission statement.
- Create a plan for your dating life, your financial life, and your future based on your mission statement.
- List some new things you'd like to try doing and begin taking steps toward doing them.
- Carve out your personal Ultimate YOU Plan and live by it. Build a strategy into making it a reality and stick to it.

The Ultimate YOU Plan Prayer

Lord, Your Word tells me that the plans You have for me are good, plans to succeed and prosper and to give me a future and hope. My hope and trust is completely in You. Let the desires of my heart line up with Your perfect will for my life. Give me wisdom and discernment regarding work, relationships, finances, and everything else that concerns me. Help me be a woman who walks in integrity and the fruit of the Holy Spirit, always being pleasing to You. I know that I can do all things with You and through You. Apart from You I can do nothing. I walk in fullness of joy knowing that I've been created with a purpose and plan in mind and believe that You will help me walk in that purpose and intent with a passionate heart. I pray it all in the name of Jesus, amen.

NOTES

Where We Are Now
1. Michelle Borquez, Connie Wetzel, Rosalind Spinks-Seay, and Carla Sue Nelson, *Live, Laugh, Love Again: A Christian Woman's Survival Guide to Divorce* (Nashville: Hachette, 2009).

Chapter 2: YOU and Forgiveness
1. R. T. Kendall, *Total Forgiveness* (Lake Mary, FL: Charisma House, 2002).

Chapter 3: YOU and Being Alone
1. Dan Buettner, *The Blue Zones* (Washington, DC: National Geographic, 2008).

Chapter 5: YOU and Sex
1. Paula Rinehart, *Sex and the Soul of a Woman* (Grand Rapids: Zondervan, 2004).

Chapter 6: YOU and Money
1. Dave Ramsey, *Financial Peace* (New York: Viking, 1997); Dave Ramsey, *The Total Money Makeover* (Nashville: Thomas Nelson, 2009).

Chapter 7: YOU and Respect

1. Melody Beattie, *The Language of Letting Go* (Center City, MN: Hazeldon, 1990).
2. *Merriam-Webster*, s.v. "respect."
3. Francine Rivers, *Redeeming Love* (Sisters, OR: Multnomah, 2007).

ACKNOWLEDGMENTS

FROM MICHELLE:

My amazing children, Joshua, Aaron, Madison, and Jacob, who walked through this difficult journey with me, I am forever grateful for each one of you. You pushed me to heal and gave me strength to press through. I love you dearly. My husband, Michael, my best friend, whose love I am in awe of, your support of me in my efforts to encourage women who have moved through the tragedy of divorce has given me such strength. Thank you to my parents who have been married for almost fifty years and who continue to show all of us that marriage is not broken, people are broken, but God's covenant and design of marriage is still a beautiful thing. To all my awesome girlfriends, especially Lisa Ostrowski, whose love and encouragement is what helped me breathe. There is nothing like friends who help hold your head high in dark moments. You all know who you are and I love each one of you. Chip MacGregor, you are more than an agent; you are a dear friend. Thank you for all your insights and mostly for your friendship all these years. To Thomas Nelson, thank you for grabbing hold of this vision and moving it forward and for believing in this book. Lord, You and You alone are the reason I live today. You were there in moments of heartache, loneliness, and despair. Your love for me, Your forgiveness of me, and Your grace in my life leave me speechless before You. I am wholly dedicated to Your purpose and to helping to heal the hearts of people who have lost their way.

FROM CONNIE:

Chip MacGregor from MacGregor Literary Agency for believing in this project and catching our vision to help women live well after divorce.

Thomas Nelson Publishing for helping us get this book out to all who can benefit from reading it.

My dear girlfriends who walked with me through each of my heartbreaks, loved me through them, held me accountable, and made me want to be a better woman. You know who you are.

To my Lord and Savior, Jesus, who continues to present opportunities for me to share and help others through my experiences. I am so grateful.

ABOUT THE AUTHORS

In 2005, Michelle hosted and co-produced I-Life Television's *Shine with Michelle Borquez* on INSP and is the creator, producer, and host of a new eight-week DVD series for women, "Live Again: Wholeness After Divorce," released in June 2013 with Aspire Publishing. Michelle is also the national spokesperson for Beth Moore's "Loving Well" television special and "GLO" Bible, and has authored several books, *Live, Laugh, Love Again, God Crazy,* and *Overcoming the Seven Deadly Emotions.* Released in 2013 are *Forever God Crazy* and *God Crazy Freedom,* and the God Crazy Freedom Series was released in stores nationwide in April 2013 in conjunction with the national "God Crazy Freedom" speaking tour. Michelle has hosted and been a featured guest on hundreds of television and radio programs, including NBC's *Midday Connection, The 700 Club, Life Today with James and Betty Robinson, Positively Texas,* and TBN, to name a few.

In 1999, Michelle founded *Shine,* a general interest women's publication highlighting articles on fashion, travel, and health. As editor-in-chief, she interviewed well-known leaders such as First Lady Laura Bush, Anne Graham Lotz, Michael W. Smith, Kurt Warner, Chuck and Gena Norris, Beth Moore, and others.

Shine published for nine years with more than forty thousand subscribers. She is also the co-owner of Ecco Bella Salon and Boutique in Franklin, TN, and of shopbellastyle.com.

Michelle is a visionary, entrepreneur, and business and media communications expert, with fifteen-plus years' experience in publishing, business development, media production, producing, directing, writing, and on-camera training. She is a results-oriented person with excellent multitasking ability, organization, and team-building skills.

Michelle lives in Nashville with her husband, author Michael Thornton, and her almost-grown four children, Joshua, Aaron, Madison, and Jacob.

• • •

Connie Wetzell is a voice over artist, singer, author, speaker, producer, and an engaging communicator. You've heard her versatile voice on numerous commercials, popular audio books, or even while you were "on hold." Her client roster ranges from Sprint, to *USA Today*, to Lowe's, The Home Depot, American Express, Enterprise Rent-A-Car, Bank of America, and a host of others. Connie received an A.I.R., *Achievement in Radio* award by the March of Dimes for having the Best Morning Show on a popular syndicated Christian Radio station in Nashville, Way-FM in 1998. It was evident then, as it is now, that Connie has the gift of humor and an eloquence in expressing the joys and sorrows of life. She is an author of *Live Laugh Love Again* (Warner Faith) and the powerful audio series, The Healing Word of God, where she poignantly delivers the words of faith, comfort, peace, and hope found in the Bible. Collaborations include, *God's Survival*

Guide, God's Survival Guide for Women (Elm Hill Books/Thomas Nelson). In addition, she has also voiced and produced *Devotionals for Women On the Go*, an audio devotional for Women of Faith. She is a contributing writer for *WHOA* magazine, a national quarterly publication for women.

Having gone through many difficulties, including life debilitating panic attacks and a devastating divorce after 26 years, she passionately and vulnerably communicates the message that through faith in God and standing on the promises of His Word, there *is* hope. Connie says, "The Word is medicine for the soul. It's the medicine that doesn't have any negative side effects. You can't overdose on it. It's guaranteed to work every time. And, it's absolutely free." Her desire is for you to know that whatever difficult circumstances you may be facing, you are not alone. Every answer for life's journey is found in God's Word.

Connie currently lives in the Bay area in Northern California close to her two daughters and two grandchildren.

SCRIPTURE INDEX

SUBJECT INDEX

A

abusers, 104, 105–106
  money and, 114
acceptance, 2, 37
  actions for, 14–20
  vs. denial, 8
  prayer, 20
  questions for considering,
  2–3
  thoughts on, 13
accountability person, 152
action plan, importance of, 155
actions
  for acceptance, 14–20
  for being alone, 61–62
  of date, 135
  for dating, 86–88
  for forgiveness, 40–41
  on money, 126
  for respect, 151–152

for sexual relationships,
111–112
  taking responsibility for, 28
alcohol, 159
aloneness, xviii, xxii, 45–61,
165–167
  actions for, 61–62
  avoiding, 46
  God and, 55
  vs. loneliness, 57
  thoughts on, 60–61
anger
  in date, 87
  with God, 35, 37
  holding on to, xvii, 22, 39
  impact of, 29, 38–39
  justifying, 21, 40
  moving past, 32
  in phone conversation, 85
  recognizing, 42
  working through, xvi

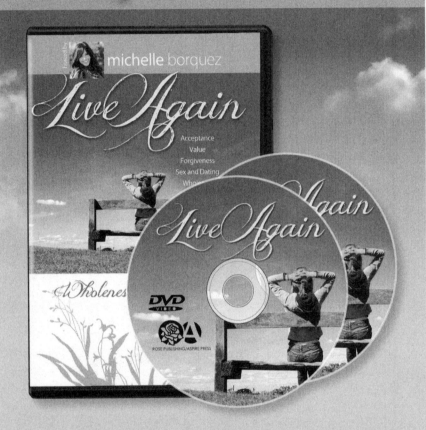